TEACH
don't
PITCH

Author's website: https://lifesciencecopywriter.com

ISBN-13: 979-8875527418
ASIN: B0CV3LRYSK

ASIN: B0CVFD2L71 (Kindle eBook)

First edition, January 2024

Book Cover by Majid Khan

Printed in the United States of America

B2B buyers want empathy. And though they hate to be sold, they love to buy!

TEACH *don't* PITCH

Tailor a continuum of empathy-based content to your buyer's search intent at every stage of the decision-making process. And transform prospects into valuable B2B leads.

Juliette R. Ongus, Ph.D.

DEDICATION

For Ian and Ethan.

TABLE OF CONTENTS

Preface

PREFACE

The year 2020 surprised everyone. It wasn't what anyone saw coming.

Locked down in my home due to the COVID-19 pandemic, I had the space to re-evaluate my priorities, self-reflect, and introspect.

It was during this time that I realized I needed to change the trajectory of my career.

But where was this nudging feeling coming from?

I had spent most of my working life, up to this point, as a faculty member at my local university. After almost two decades of the same routine, I had acclimatized to a certain rhythm, which started with the admission of students at the beginning of every academic year.

So I guess it was the right time to ask …

What if I could experience something different?

I was ready. It was time to shift gears. I looked back to my childhood for the familiar. What did my mother do when faced with the chance to change course?

Sadly, I recalled watching her let opportunities slip by. And how much she regretted not making good use of the chances life had thrown her way.

I remembered promising myself never to repeat her mistakes. Never to create a situation that would make me look back on lost opportunities in regret.

The lockdown was my opportune moment. To master a new skill. To reinvent my career.

All I knew was that I wanted to do something new that excited and inspired me. But what was it exactly?

As an introvert, I felt drawn to digital marketing … whatever that meant.

So I went searching for answers where everyone goes. Google. But I didn't know what to look for. All I knew was that I wanted to find something that required my intellectual input.

After a few searches, I stumbled upon this strange word: 'copywriting'.

I had heard of copyrights. Was it the legal stuff? Had they meant to spell it 'copyrighting' … as in copyright?

But I am a scientist. No! I wasn't interested in legal matters.

However, the more I searched for digital marketing, the more this strange, misspelled word 'copywriting' kept popping up. So I thought … Why not search for 'copywriting' instead?

Now, what came up was interesting. I wanted to know more about it. The more I read about copywriting, the more I liked what I found. And eventually, I understood that copywriting was the sales language in print.

Sales?

Another flashback, but this time to my early adult years. My first job was as a salesperson. I was so bad at it. Sales wasn't my thing. And that did not get better later. Every business opportunity I tried failed because I did not know how to sell.

But what I read about copywriting fascinated me. It promised to equip me with the tools to be effective at sales. All I had to do was learn the principles of persuasive writing.

Of course, I could do that! I'd be in business if I could learn how to write this language. And help others be good at sales.

Another Google search. But this time for copywriting training.

And there it was … American Writers and Artists Institute (AWAI).

I clicked on the link and landed on their website. After reviewing it, I enrolled in the B2B Copywriting Mastery program and never looked back. That started my professional career as a B2B copywriter.

And as Winston Churchill once said, "*Everybody stumbles across a golden opportunity at least once in their lifetime.*" I was incredibly fortunate to stumble upon copywriting.

What about this book?

The inspiration to write it came from Nick Usborne ... one of my AWAI copywriting instructors. During one of his digital copywriting classes, he dared us to write books. That was in 2021, during the COVID-19 lockdown.

And these were his exact words ...

"It's hard to build a successful career as a copywriter if you just take baby steps. What bigger thing can you do to stand out from the rest? Something bigger that will make you jump out of the crowd."

He went on to say ...

"As you seek to build your career in a noisy space, you must do something different. Something that will improve the perception of the value that you bring to the table. And from my personal experience, I found that investing in writing a book helped kick things into a whole new gear."

That's where my journey to writing this book started. A dare.

But how did I kick the writing process off?

While most people start writing books by creating a MindMup, that didn't work for me. It left me feeling confined, restricted, and not creative. But I gave it a try anyway. I pushed through my discomfort and wrote the first two chapters.

Or so I thought ...

It took me one year to complete the first draft. And as I pen this preface, those two initial chapters do not appear anywhere in this book. They ended up being ... what I now call ... 'warm-up copy'.

Anyway ... this book aims to simplify the fundamental concepts of crafting compelling B2B content.

I delve into the core principles of strategy, audience analysis, and empathy. Tactics that will empower you to create impactful content that drives business growth. I also look at content production, distribution channels, and the metrics to measure success.

The content of each chapter was curated with information from research, published papers, interactions with clients, and my professional knowledge.

I offer practical tips for a well-rounded perspective that you can apply to mount your own B2B campaigns.

As I present this work to the world, I hope it inspires you to become a better content marketer.

~ Juliette R. Ongus, Ph.D.
Founder, Life Science Copywriter.

Prologue

Consumer Psychology and Organizational Buyer Behavior

CHAPTER ONE

The Subconscious Mind in Organizational Buying Decision-Making

Quote

"95% of purchase decision-making takes place in the subconscious mind."

~ Gerald Zaltman ~
Professor, Harvard Business School.

The buying decision-making process is intricate, subjective, and influenced by numerous factors that vary from person to person. So when your buyers have several products to choose from, they often have to pick the best one. But how would they determine which one is best?

A growing body of research suggests that complex cognitive processes drive consumer behavior by influencing how the mind processes information to arrive at buying decisions.

These processes include evaluating alternatives, weighing pros and cons, and determining the perceived value of your product or service.

In many organizations that rely on multiple people to make purchase decisions, it gets even more complex.

Thus, as a B2B marketer, you have to understand the different states of human consciousness. Understanding subconscious drivers of consumer behavior can equip you with greater awareness of your buyer's needs, which is crucial for creating compelling marketing and sales content.

It will also give you a profound understanding of your target audience's experiences, which will enable you to show empathy in your messaging.

So the answer to how buyers determine which product is best lies in understanding the subjective biases that influence them to choose one product or service over another.

Let's Start By Looking At Three Levels Of Human Consciousness ...

1. *The Unconscious Mind:*
   Unconsciousness is the most basic level of human consciousness. It holds past events and memories. It is inaccessible to us, no matter how hard we try to remember to bring things up. And it functions on autopilot. In the unconscious mind, people react instinctively to environmental stimuli ... with innate impulses and conditioned responses. This is where actions and decisions happen remotely without conscious awareness.

2. *The Conscious Mind:*
   The conscious mind is a state where people are fully awakened to the reality of things happening in the present. They engage in self-reflection

and introspection, make deliberate choices, and exercise critical thinking. In this state, they don't need to rely on memorized information. Because they engage with events in their surroundings in real time, so you can use things in the current moment to trigger their actions.

3. *The Subconscious Mind:*
This is where memories, emotions, thoughts, beliefs, and behaviors reside. It holds information beneath our conscious awareness and is often associated with intuition. It defines reactions and automatic actions. It is always working in the background, but people are not necessarily aware of it. But one can become aware of it if they think about it. It contains all the stored information about everything a person has ever experienced. So you can tap into it to influence behavior, thoughts, and how your audience acts.

Of the three levels of human consciousness, the conscious mind drives rational behavior, while the subconscious mind holds our thoughts and emotions.

On the one hand, rational drivers are logical and objective. They rely on practical considerations that depend on reasoning.

On the other hand, emotional drivers are subjective. They include personal preferences, feelings, and desires.

The Rise of Conscious Consumerism

Human consciousness shapes consumer behavior by influencing product perceptions and preferences.

Consumer psychologists now agree that emotional and rational drivers are elements of behavior that, when aligned, can influence consumer buying decisions.

According to the copywriter Eugene M. Schwartz, emotions are natural forces of the subconscious mind. Our hopes, dreams, fears, and desires contribute significantly to *"mass desire"* ... what he described as *"the public spread of a private want"*.

And the driving force that makes content marketing work comes from the audience, not the content itself.

Emotions drive consumer behavior by simplifying buying decision-making. And lay the foundation for making snap judgments about whether to buy.

So, as a marketer, you cannot create "*mass desire*" for your products because it's already there. Just waiting to be satisfied.

People are now seeking products and services that resonate with their values. This has led to conscious consumerism gaining momentum as buyers become increasingly conscious of their choices.

And as more people become aware of the social, environmental, and ethical implications of their purchasing decisions, you must adapt your strategies and align them with the evolving consumer consciousness to remain relevant in a dynamic marketplace.

This paradigm shift is driving many businesses to adopt sustainable practices, promote transparency, and prioritize social impact to attract and retain conscious consumers.

Later in this book, we will cover different ways to delve into your buyer's subconscious mind to gain valuable insights into their motivations and emotions. This is how you can create content that improves their experiences and connects their hopes, dreams, fears, desires, and emotions to your product.

Emotional And Rational Drivers Of Organizational Buying Decision-Making

In business-to-business (B2B) organizations, the 'Decision-Making Unit' makes purchase decisions.

This is the team of people tasked with making buying decisions on behalf of the organization. They sit at the table with individual roles and biases. And their choices are neither solely rational nor logical.

So, for your content to perform effectively, you should be familiar with organizational psychology and consumer behavior.

Here's why ...

Gerald Zaltman, a professor at Harvard Business School, says ... *"95% of our purchase decision-making takes place in the subconscious mind"*.

In his book, *"How Customers Think: Essential Insights into the Mind of the Market,"* he says ... *"Consumers are driven by subconscious urges, the biggest of which is emotion"*.

So, if we go by Professor Zaltman's hypothesis, the most effective way to appeal to the subconscious mind is to engage your buyer's emotions.

Why?

Because both emotional and rational motivations influence every B2B purchase decision.

And you should anticipate that your buyers will not buy for rational reasons alone. Instead, they use logic to justify why their emotional reasons for purchasing are valid.

Subconscious emotional biases underlie the buying decision-making process. And the people making organizational buying decisions cannot separate themselves from their feelings.

On one axis, the B2B decision-making process involves opposing individual-level and company-level needs. On the other axis, there are competing emotional and rational motivations.

So if you want your buyers to interact with your brand in an engaged and passionate way, sell them happy feelings. And over time, they can associate your products with those happy feelings.

The key here is to move them away from their pain as you encourage them to associate your products with good feelings.

This will connect them to your brand and make them loyal.

Individual-Level Needs Are More Emotional

On an individual level, the emotional drivers of the buying process are all about personal relationships. It's about ...

- The quality of their interactions with sales representatives.
- The quality of customer service.
- The extent to which sales representatives understand their industry.
- How sales representatives respond to queries, listen to their needs, and
- The terms of delivery, like free delivery, same-day delivery, etc.

At the personal level, the stakes are higher. This is where you will find that if your buyers make the wrong decision, they can lose their jobs. So they need your product or service to help them make the right decision.

And because many people think that change is risky, you will encounter a lot of status quo bias. So you have to overcome that to sell your product to them.

Another thing you will notice about the individual-level decision-making criteria is loss aversion.

Your buyers are more likely to act in ways that prevent losses than make choices that bring gains. So you must present your product from the correct perspective to overcome this and rationalize its worth.

It will also not be unusual to observe decision paralysis. Especially when a large number of people are involved in decision-making. And so, the larger the 'Decision-Making Unit', the less likely it will be for them to reach a consensus.

The role of your content here is to help them make easy decisions more quickly. And your product or service must meet specific functional needs to be on the shortlist.

Even though individual-level needs are more emotional, the 'Decision-Making Unit' also leans on rational motivations to drive buying decisions. These include …
- Reduced training time. B2B users prioritize ease of use because it ensures a shorter but smoother implementation.
- Efficiency. They want to boost their productivity when using your product.
- Convenience. They want it to be easy to set up or install your product.
- Guarantees. They need product warranties and after-sales service to reduce their risk.

Organizational-Level Needs Are More Rational

At the company level, rationality is built into purchase decisions. And generally, organizational purchases tend to be more structured and well-justified.

So, at the company level, rational drivers of the buying decision criteria can be divided into 4 …

1. *Technical aspects that specify how 'fit for purpose' the product is.*
   This concerns …
   - Product quality or reliability.
   - Product durability, performance, and functionality.
   - How easily the product integrates with the organization's infrastructure, and
   - How product specifications comply with the required standards.

2. *Financial aspects of the product:*
   This is about …
   - The price or cost. The most important decision driver across all industry segments.
   - Pricing models that help reduce the burden of substantial upfront costs.
   - Payment terms (e.g., subscription, installments, or payment plans), and
   - The cost of general maintenance.

3. *Business aspects of the product:*
   These are …
   - Cost-effectiveness or value for money.
   - Increase in sales or market share, and
   - Return on investment (ROI), such as 5X.

4. *Legal aspects of the product:*
   Such as …
   - Adherence to regulations.
   - Ease of doing business, and
   - Acceptance of paperwork.

Even though organizational-level needs are more rational, they also have emotional drivers for buying decisions. They are all about brand reputation and include …

- Customer reviews.
- Star ratings.
- Order fulfillment rate, and
- Turnaround time (TAT).

Coming Up In The Next Chapter …

The Allure Of Empathy In Content Marketing.

CHAPTER TWO

The Allure of Empathy in Content Marketing

$$Quote$$

"B2B buyers want empathy, not empty promises. They don't turn off their consumer brains when making organizational purchases".

~ April Henderson ~
VP and Consulting Director at Forrester Research, Inc.

People love to buy. But they don't know what they need. They hate being sold to because it gives them the impression that they are being told what to do. And they don't like that.

But when you explain the 'why' behind your products or services, you can significantly impact the success of your marketing efforts. Because the reason 'why' clearly articulates the purpose, values, and unique selling points of your product or service.

In other words, it provides a compelling reason to buy by creating a strong emotional connection that resonates deeply with your buyers.

Here's why …

If you can show them why your product is important to them, it will help them understand the value you bring. That's because it all comes down to providing value to your audience instead of simply trying to sell them something.

The Need To Know The Reason 'Why' Is A Fundamental Human Desire

In 1978, Ellen Jane Langer … a psychology professor at Harvard University, conducted research on a college campus where people usually lined up to use a busy copy machine.

She wanted to know what would happen if random people asked to jump the line and go to the front of the queue.

So she set up her experiment to have 3 groups, each of which received a distinctly different but specifically worded request.

The first group was instructed to ask, *"Excuse me, I have 5 pages. May I use the Xerox machine?"*

The second group was told to ask, *"Excuse me, I have 5 pages. May I use the Xerox machine? BECAUSE I have to make copies."*

And the third group asked, *"Excuse me, I have 5 pages. May I use the Xerox machine? BECAUSE I'm in a rush."*

When she looked at the results, she found that the first group got 60%

compliance. The lowest recorded in the study.

To her surprise, the second group got 93% compliance, and the third group got 94% compliance.

She concluded that stating any reason with the word 'because' significantly increased compliance. The word 'because' was the magic that got almost everyone in the study to comply without offering resistance.

And that remained true even when the justification for the request wasn't compelling.

Here's why …

The need to know the reason 'why' is a fundamental human desire. And from a very early age, people want to know 'why'.

Knowing 'why' helps us understand the reasons behind anything before we do it. Knowing 'why' allows us to make decisions in the absence of direction. And when we know 'why', we'll be comfortable enough to lay down our objections.

That's exactly where you want your buyers to be … to lay down their objections and purchase your product.

However, when explanations aren't forthcoming, poor outcomes ensue.

And so, as a marketer, explaining why your product is the best solution for their problem should be the key message your content delivers. So focus on the reason ... not the pitch. That's what will make your content valuable to your prospects.

However, how they weigh their purchase options after that depends on the urgency of their need. But they're far more likely to accept your offer if they understand the reason 'why'.

Empathy Is The Secret Behind Compelling Content That Drives B2B Sales

It's not uncommon for people to search for solutions to their problems online. And every time they submit a query, algorithms capture and analyze their data.

This makes it easy for you to tap into the data to understand what content your target audience is searching for.

However, information isn't the only thing that matters to them. So being overly data-centric or relying on AI-generated content can create a disconnect between you and them.

Why?

Because your audience is made up of real humans, not data points.

According to April Henderson, VP and Consulting Director at Forrester Research, Inc. ... *"B2B buyers want empathy, not empty promises. They don't turn off their consumer brains when making organizational purchases"*.

So now that you know that B2B buyers expect personalized content with a more individualized approach, how can you deliver that?

As a business owner or content marketer, it's no longer enough to think like your buyer. The only way to hit the bull's eye with your marketing content is to BE the buyer. But how can you BE the buyer?

The keyword here is empathy.

Empathy is the capacity to see your buyer's perspective and be part of their experience as they navigate your marketing funnel.

But how can you give them personalized content that equips them to make an informed judgment at each step on a consistent and ongoing basis?

You must first put yourself in their place to see their perspective, feel their pain, and identify with the challenges they face.

In a later chapter of this book, we will see how you can use a buyer persona matrix to discover the specific challenges each member of the Decision-Making Unit is facing.

And how that information can guide you to tailor content that speaks directly to their challenges, needs, and interests at each stage of the buying decision-making process.

But remember, the purpose of content marketing is to help you forge a deep emotional connection with them. So you want to match the information in your content to their needs at each stage.

So, when your content is infused with empathy, it allows you to humanize your brand. And it makes you come across as more relatable, genuinely wanting to help, and approachable to your audience.

It also offers insightful solutions that resonate with your buyer's unique concerns. It addresses their specific fears, frustrations, or aspirations. It contains enough information and depth to leave a lasting impression.

Not only that …

Approaching content marketing with empathy will differentiate your brand. It allows you to create content that is not only informative but also emotionally engaging.

And in the long run, empathy-based content builds trust. It resonates with your target audience and generates a sense of loyalty among customers. It connects your prospects to your brand and makes them derive genuine satisfaction from your product.

This encourages them to be more receptive to your messaging, which impacts their intent to buy and delivers real business results.

Coming Up In The Next Chapter …

PART 1: The Fundamentals of a B2B Content Strategy

Part 1

The Fundamentals of a B2B Content Strategy

CHAPTER THREE

A Business Case For Your Content Marketing Strategy

Quote

"A goal without a plan
is just a wish".

~ Antoine de Saint-Exupéry ~
Writer and Pioneering Aviator.

The COVID-19 lockdown in 2020 accelerated the surge in interest in digital marketing in modern times. And for the first time, the only way businesses could reach their prospects was through digital content. That shifted the perception of content marketing from being an exciting concept to being a necessary survival tactic that every business needed to adopt.

And today, pretty much every business is looking for quality content to reach their target audience.

So the argument in favor of content marketing has certainly taken root. There is undeniable evidence that it should be prioritized.

But the hardest part for marketers remains getting the coveted executive buy-in. Or, more specifically, having a dedicated budget allocated for it.

Why?

For many business organizations, project justification usually takes a commercial form. And marketing dollars must be spent wisely. So you know that you cannot simply submit ideas to the C-Suite and expect to get automatic approval.

Thus, every 'new' suggestion is rightfully met with at least a little skepticism from senior executives.

They will reject proposals when they have the impression that marketing is trying to sell something to them.

That's why 22% of B2B marketers … interviewed for the "*Research Insights*" report compiled by the Content Marketing Institute … considered the failure to get executive buy-in the greatest barrier to implementing a content strategy.

The Rationale for Getting Executive Buy-In for Your Content Marketing

Without executive engagement, priorities in the organization can shift rapidly.

And as Joe Pulizzi … the author of Epic Content Marketing and founder of the Content Marketing Institute … said, "*It becomes difficult to get the right teams involved*".

It also becomes difficult to have specific tactics approved or get permission to experiment. To learn from mistakes or make necessary changes that can bring about future success.

But how can you turn this around?

By preparing a well-researched business case. This has become a prerequisite for getting any content marketing initiatives off the ground.

Rather than merely asking for budgetary support, you must demonstrate the risks and rewards of your strategic direction ... and most importantly ... the expected return on investment (ROI).

What is a Business Case?

A business case is an abbreviated proposal that outlines the justification for undertaking a project.

In the case of content marketing, it's a tool that compares content marketing to alternative options in a way that senior management can use to base their decision-making. It outlines the risks and benefits, the cost of the investment, and a rationale for the preferred solution.

In the case of content marketing, it also initiates discussions about the required funding for a potential portfolio.

A business case also allows you to critically examine alternatives. It outlines the financial implications of your content marketing strategy ... and improves your chances of winning approvals.

So you have to think of it as a sales pitch.

You have to provide robust analysis and justification for your strategy. And since there's so much at stake, you should perfect your pitch.

A 3-Step Framework to Build a Business Case for Your Content Marketing

The goal is to convince senior management to approve the investment you are requesting.

And there's no shortage of market research data that shows the effectiveness of a well-executed content marketing strategy. So make sure you do your homework because you can easily prove that your plan deserves resources.

But remember, your business case is a summary, not a seminar. And to make it as effective as possible, it must be tight and to the point.

A convincing rationale for senior management must have three core components:

STEP #1: *Provide Market Research Data Necessary To Underpin What Content Marketing Could Do For Your Business.*

You want to lay the foundation for using content marketing. That shouldn't be difficult to do because there is an abundance of information available from secondary sources that presents content marketing in a positive light.

However, don't take those facts and figures wholesale and present them directly to senior management. Because using such an approach often invites suspicion … right from the beginning.

A better way is to present a clear and compelling case based on a sound understanding of the core principles and benefits of content marketing. And you can match these against the opportunities your organization wants to pursue.

So focus on showing how audience attention and habits are shifting … and why that matters. And of course, the changing dynamics of your audience are only part of the problem. The publishing and advertising landscapes are also shifting.

It helps to reference credible research that shows relevant trends in marketing.

Here are 4 ideas you may want to pursue as you develop the foundation for your business case.

1. *Content impacts the entire marketing and sales pipeline.*
   And as more people spend time online, audiences want relationships with brands ... not a bombardment of advertising.

2. *Many people spend time on social media platforms.*
   So you need to populate your owned, earned, and paid media channels to drive your business goals.

3. *Social targeting performs better when it leverages relevant content.*
   Sophisticated social targeting can enable you to reach your target audiences ... without breaking your marketing budget.

4. *Traditional ways of advertising aren't working as well as they used to.*
   The cost of reaching audiences through each channel using paid ads continues to rise. And as advertising noise increases, consumers are using technology to block ads.

STEP #2: *Model What Content Marketing Will Look Like For Your Business.*

Painting a vision of success isn't enough. You must also show tangible proof of the concept.

What are your plans for the following 3 to 5 years after the launch?

You need to identify the marketing goals that your company must achieve. You also need to figure out how content marketing will bring you closer to that.

There are many competing factors to take into account when making a decision. And it's not always easy to figure out which should take priority.

The best way to figure this out is to ask the following questions:

- What are some of the ways that a content marketing strategy might deliver better results from your digital channels?
- How would additional traffic to your site contribute to your top-of-the-funnel pipeline?
- Would additional traffic result in a greater number of potential sales opportunities?
- What would be the impact of having better-quality leads on sales?
- How will content marketing bring you closer to your Key Performance Indicators (KPIs) and financial outcomes?

When faced with several variables, a decision matrix can highlight what you need to factor into your proposal. This can clear up the confusion by bringing related information closer to each other ... and helping you uncover actionable insights that will then impact your end goal.

A decision matrix is a multi-variable grid that compares marketing alternatives. It analyzes resource requirements, costs, and the expected return on investment. It can help you craft arguments to defend a decision you've already made.

It is a quantitative approach that removes subjectivity by assessing a situation from a logical perspective. It removes emotion and can help you make a compelling case for choosing content marketing.

Also, you can easily justify how it aligns with your organization's strategic goals.

Ideally, you should bring to the discussion a robust cost-benefit analysis to back up your proposal. And summarize the results into a decision matrix for that perfect finishing touch to your business case.

Once you factor all variables into your matrix, it should look like Table 3.1 ...

Table 3.1: The Business Case Template

		MARKETING ALTERNATIVES		
		Print Advertising	*Online Ads (Pay-per-click)*	*Content Marketing*
Resource Requirements	*Team Members (project lead, editorial team, and web development)*			
	New Hires (writers, editors, SEO experts, web developers, or graphic designers)			
	Project Duration:			
Risks	*Distribution*			
	Branding			
	Customer experience			
Cost	*Necessary tools or software*			
	Number of placements/Year			
	Outside agency fees			
	Team member time/Year			
	New team members/Year			
	Quarterly or yearly spends			
Expected Return on Investment	*Organic search traffic*			
	All traffic			
	Leads from the website			
	Leads from email			
	Leads from social media e.g. LinkedIn			
	Avg. $/Lead			
	Revenue Goal			

A decision matrix is particularly useful when you have several alternatives to choose from … and many variables to compare.

You could always add more variables to the matrix to customize your unique experience.

STEP #3: *Prepare A Convincing Rationale That Aligns Your Content Marketing Strategy To Your Business Goals.*

Content marketing is a strategy for brand recognition, lead generation, and customer retention. Marketers use it to get the word out, bring in traffic, get leads, and turn prospects into customers.

A convincing rationale must demonstrate how your content strategy will serve the organization's bottom line. You must justify why content marketing should be part of the organization's strategic approach.

Start small, with a pilot program to prove its effectiveness. Then build, test, and refine your assumptions.

And as the results come in, you can determine where to spend your resources.

The Key Takeaways from Chapter 13:

1. Failure to get executive buy-in is the greatest barrier to implementing a content strategy.

2. A business case is a tool that compares content marketing to alternative options in a way that senior management can use to base their decision-making.

3. A business case allows you to critically examine alternatives. It outlines the financial implications of your content marketing strategy … and improves your chances of winning approvals.

Coming Up In The Next Chapter …

Content Marketing Goals That Produce Real Business Results.

CHAPTER FOUR

Content Marketing Goals That Produce Real Business Results

Quote

"One of the best ways to
sabotage your content is to
not tie it to your goals".

~ Ellen Gomes ~
Sr. Content Marketing Manager, Glint Inc.

Too many organizations don't appreciate the business value of content marketing. Many perceive content marketing as pretty pictures with fluffy words. Or think of it as just noise ... something with no tangible or quantifiable results.

That's simply not true.

Without well-defined objectives, neither you nor your prospects will get the most out of your content marketing.

The Business Value Of Content Marketing

Content marketing influences your buyer's experience. So it is not something you want to jump into blindly. You need to think carefully about your strategy if you want your content to give your potential buyers a good experience.

You want to create a continuous stream of customer-centric content that will help your buyers decide whether or not to buy at every step of the buyer's journey.

That's why you want to show empathy for your buyers and equip them to make informed choices.

And yes ... you also want your content to generate real business results!

Ellen Gomes, Sr. Content Marketing Manager at Glint Inc. says ... *"One of the best ways to sabotage your marketing efforts is to not tie your strategy to your business goals"*.

Unfortunately, too many businesses jump into content marketing without having a strategy.

Though there are different content marketing goals, you should align each goal with a specific stage of the buying decision process. This will allow you to create targeted content that matches your buyer's search intent. It will also help you achieve your business objectives.

Ultimately, this is what will generate business results and drive growth.

So, before you start any content marketing campaign, you need to consider the bigger picture.

If you don't know the stage of the buying decision-making process where your content should serve your prospects, you risk sending out irrelevant messages that add no value to the buyer's journey.

Essentially, you will be wasting resources and time pursuing a vanity project that will not generate results.

But if you aim for a holistic content strategy that aligns your buyer's needs with your business goals, you should be able to generate real, tangible results.

To do this, you must anticipate your buyers' search intent as they go online to look for information that will help them decide whether or not to buy. Then, use your content to move them forward through each stage of your sales funnel.

This explains why many companies create a variety of content assets and spread them across the buyer's journey.

Below are 10 prioritized content marketing goals. They are purposefully selected to support each stage of the purchase decision-making process.

10 Prioritized Content Marketing Goals That Drive Real Business Results

For your content marketing strategy to be effective, you need different types of content for different stages of your marketing funnel. So it goes without saying that the objective of your content marketing strategy will depend on the stage of the buying decision-making process where your buyers are.

And so, setting goals for each stage will give your content marketing strategy direction.

The key here is to create content that aligns with your target audience's needs and interests at each stage. To move them along your sales funnel. And ultimately guide them toward conversion and retention.

At the top of the funnel (TOFU), you only have a target audience in mind. You have not interacted with these people yet. They don't know your brand.

Your interest at this stage is to draw their attention and convince them that your brand has something valuable to offer them.

Here are the 3 goals your content should aim to achieve at this top stage.

Goal #1: *To Influence Your Potential Buyer's Problem Recognition.*

> Your potential buyers are in the first decision-making stage. They are unaware of the problem they have.
>
> As a marketer, you have to deal with their apathy. And if you want them to buy anything from you, help them see this need. That way, you will get them to care about your marketing message.
>
> Why?
>
> Because recognizing their problem is the first step in the decision-making process. Problem recognition ... also called problem identification ... happens when your buyers discover their unmet needs.
>
> The best way to get them to consume your content is to use a marketing hook that speaks to their pain points or hits a desire within them.
>
> A hook is a marketing technique used to get people's attention, get them interested, and make them open to what you have to say. In other words, it gets your foot in the door.
>
> But grabbing your potential buyer's attention is one of the toughest jobs in marketing. If you want to be competitive, your marketing hook needs to stand out from the crowd. It should have a polarizing message that sides strongly with your buyers' opinions, rejects the status quo, and is authentic.

Goal #2: *To Boost Your Visibility Online By Incorporating Search Engine Optimization (SEO) Techniques.*

> In the second stage of the decision-making process, your buyers experience a psychological trigger. This enables them to recognize that they have a problem. They become interested in taking action,

so they search online for information that will help them solve this problem.

This is the content marketing goal that you're probably most familiar with … because it's the bread and butter of Search Engine Optimization (SEO).

So, when your buyers type search queries in Google, the algorithm will give them the most relevant results based on the keywords they used. Your content will rank well if those keywords are present in your text. Not only are you sharing content to help your buyers, but you're also introducing them to your brand.

But be aware of stuffing your content with keywords for high ranking. This will appear to be clickbait and may damage your domain's reputation.

You want your content to rank more easily for relevant keywords and also build your reputation with search engines. This is a key ingredient for building your domain authority and making your site more competitive.

And domain authority will extend to your email reputation, product pages, and landing pages.

Goal #3: *To Increase Your Brand's Awareness.*

In the third stage of the decision-making process, your buyers want to learn more about your brand. Brand awareness will enable them to recognize and remember your business. So you want to make a good first impression. This keeps you top-of-mind when they are making critical buying decisions.

Creating brand awareness is a common goal, especially in niche markets. You can quickly reach a relatively large audience if you show how your company can help.

You also showcase your company's expertise and knowledge when you share high-quality content. Ensure that your content uses the fonts and colors of your brand and that your logo is in a prominent place.

Now that you are done with the top of the funnel, you enter the middle-of-the-funnel (MOFU). This is where you're interested in building relationships with your prospects. You want to endear your brand to them. This is where your focus should shift to engaging, educating, and entertaining your prospects. You have 2 main goals at this stage.

Goal #4: *To Generate Consumer Demand For Your Products.*

Your buyers don't always believe what you ... the business owner ... claim or have to say about your own products and services.

They want to figure out what they need from a product and compare the available options. They want to explore your promises and support them with evidence. They also want to eliminate solutions that aren't a good fit.

And so in the fourth decision-making stage, they will go all out to conduct research online.

But don't take it personally. It's a sign of the times.

This is where you have to start leveraging belief-builders in your marketing communications.

How?

Using social proof.

Sometimes, creating the demand to buy your product is as simple as tapping into your customers' experiences to allow them to do the selling for you.

Thus, consumer-generated content will play an important role at this stage ... in providing organic, unbiased, and authentic social proof. This will reassure your buyers when making purchase decisions.

You can also reach new audiences by repurposing your original research data into educational content. Curate your data into multiple content formats. Teach your audience new ways of using your existing products.

Finally, you can use thought leadership content from a subject-matter expert in your field to boost your reputation. This will help you position your brand as a recognized authority.

Goal #5: *To Engage Your Buyers And Show Concern For Their Needs.*

In the fifth decision-making stage, your buyers want to build an emotional bond and connect with your brand.

So responding to comments on posts is an opportunity to connect on a human level. This type of engagement humanizes your company ... giving it a personality.

Why?

Because people want to buy from other people ... not brands. In the same way, people want to do business with other people ... not with companies.

Aim to create an emotional bond with your prospects by giving your brand a distinct personality.

Share information and opinions about the people behind your company.

This is an excellent way to show your human side and will lower the barrier when the time to make personal contact comes.

Once you're done with the middle of the funnel, your next stop is at the bottom of the funnel (BOFU). This is where you'll leverage content to convert prospects into paying customers.

Bottom-of-funnel content is different from content used in earlier stages. Rather than build trust, you'll focus on persuasive content assets to convert your leads into paying customers.

You have 3 goals to achieve here.

Goal #6: *To Generate Leads By Offering A Valuable Lead Magnet.*

At the sixth stage of the decision-making process, your buyers think your lead magnet is very valuable. It promises immediate gratification by focusing on their problem.

You can collect user information in exchange for access because this content is gated. Your potential customers are happy to give you their contact information in exchange for a demo or access to your lead magnet. So now you can grow your email list.

It is important to remember that content in this category is closer to revenue. And even though it brings in less traffic, the traffic is of higher quality. You can use this content to support your sales team.

Goal #7: *To Overcome Common Sales Objections.*

In the seventh stage of the decision-making process, your buyers may experience feelings of doubt and may need reassurance. They need social proof to move beyond their doubts, overcome their objections, and find answers to their questions.

To improve their experience, you must follow up with nurturing email messages. The ultimate goal of lead nurturing is to achieve a sale. So use relevant content to build trust. This will make it much easier to convert them later.

They need support to screen suppliers and make a vendor selection.

So at this stage, your content should help your buyers overcome their objections. And one of the most common objections involves price hesitation. You may also find people who don't understand how your products are better than those of your competitors.

Both consumers and business buyers tend to be suspicious of marketing claims in ads, websites, emails, and other communication forms.

But business buyers are even more skeptical.

They're not impressed by vague claims of 'outstanding quality' or 'months of uptime between maintenance periods'.

They want evidence. Facts. Specifics. Proof.

And the way you give that proof is to integrate belief-builders into your message.

What's a belief-builder?

Any information that backs your claim and provides solid evidence that your readers can rely on to believe your message.

Goal #8: *To Generate Sales Revenue By Closing More Deals.*

In the eighth decision-making stage, your buyers are pretty close to making a purchase decision. They discover an aspect of your product they didn't expect. And from here on, they can't live without it.

They commit to buying and only need to find a reason to justify becoming paying customers.

At this stage, your sole focus is revenue generation.

Adding proof points to your sales message will help them see why they should buy your product or service.

So focus on creating content assets with one goal in mind ... to move your buyers even closer to purchasing your products.

After the bottom of the funnel, you enter the final stage of your sales funnel ... the revenue optimization of the funnel (ROFU). You are now dealing with your paying clients.

At this stage, the goal of your content is to help you scale your business. So you want to support your company's growth through repeat business and referrals.

You have 2 final goals to achieve here.

Goal #9: *To Increase Your Customer Lifetime Value By Boosting Retention &*
Loyalty.

In the ninth decision-making stage, your buyers are in the post-
purchase experience phase of the buyer's journey. Your first-time
buyers are getting to know how well the product works. They will
review its performance and may want to consult your resources for
help.

Be empathetic and put yourself in their shoes. Provide helpful
resources where customer service gaps exist.

And after they buy, you can find opportunities to sell MORE.
Offer different possibilities. Perhaps an upsell or a cross-sell.

But don't forget to ask, because repeat purchases are key to
improved customer retention.

Repeat buyers don't come with any costs associated with new
customer acquisition. You can turn your one-time buyers into loyal
customers when you remarket to them.

And if you can encourage your customers to buy your products
more often, you can make more money and expand your profit
margin.

Goal #10: *To Turn Your Customers Into Brand Advocates By Offering Incentives*
They Can Use To Bring In Referrals.

In the tenth decision-making stage, your buyers appreciate the great
experience they had using your product. They become brand
advocates whenever they share your solutions with their peers.

The ultimate goal of your brand should be to create evangelists.
These are people who are excited to share good things about your
company or product.

And if you provide them with shareable content pieces, they can
easily reach others and drive up interest in your offer.

But you have to take care of your evangelists, for if you disappoint
them, they can quickly become your worst critics.

The Key Takeaways from Chapter 3:

1. The business purpose of content marketing must not be lost. You must align your strategy with your business objectives to generate tangible results.

2. You should align each goal with a specific stage of the buying decision process. This will allow you to create targeted content that matches your buyer's search intent.

3. If you don't know the decision stage where your marketing content should serve, you risk creating content with the wrong objective in mind.

Coming Up In The Next Chapter …

Part 2: 6 Pillars of an Empathy-Based Content Strategy

Part 2

6 Pillars of an Empathy-Based Content Strategy

CHAPTER FIVE

Pillar #1: Brand 'Voice' … Your Brand's Personality Framework

$$\mathcal{Q}uote$$

"Your brand is a story
unfolding across all customer
touchpoints".

*~ **Jonah Sachs** ~*
Author, Speaker, and Viral Marketer

Accrording to Gerald Zaltman ... a professor at Harvard Business School ... *"95% of our purchase decision-making takes place in the subconscious mind"*. In his book, *"How Customers Think: Essential Insights into the Mind of the Market,"* he says ... *"Consumers are driven by subconscious urges, the biggest of which is emotion"*.

How can your brand elicit a positive emotional response from your buyers?

One effective way for your brand to increase its equity is by creating a personality for it ... what is also known as Brand 'Voice'.

Brand 'Voice' is a set of human characteristics attributed to your brand that offer consistent qualitative value-added traits that elicit a positive emotional response from your buyers.

So, if we go by Professor Zaltman's hypothesis, the most effective way to engage your buyer's emotions is to appeal to the subconscious mind.

Your brand 'Voice' does that by impacting how your entire brand is identified.

It will help you develop communication styles to reach your target audience clearly, influence how your market perceives you, and help your buyers bond with your products.

In this chapter, we will explore the key elements of a brand 'Voice' and discuss best practices to craft a compelling and impactful brand persona.

We will see how you can refer to two of the most popular brand personality frameworks on the market to tailor yours. That is ...

1. Carl Jung's 12 brand personality archetypes, and
2. Jennifer Aaker's 5 brand personality frameworks.

Carl Jung's 12 Brand Personality Archetypes

In 1919, Carl Jung ... a Swiss psychologist ... described 12 brand personality archetypes.

Understanding where your brand falls in this scheme is a powerful way to know how best to position your brand in your target market.

Table 5.1: Carl Jung's Brand Archetype #1: CREATOR or ARTIST.

Dominant Traits:	Imaginative. Nonconformist. Expression. Vision. Originality. Individualism.
Desire:	To be the first to realize an idea, introduce new technologies, or create unique combinations of features. To create something with meaning and enduring value by pushing the limits of design.
Core Values:	Innovation.
Drivers:	Building solutions that don't exist. Giving customers the freedom to create and express themselves.
Greatest Fear:	To be inauthentic and mediocre.
Target Audience:	They're not fans of traditional advertising or mediocre products with features that already exist. But they will pay a premium price for products that inspire them.
Example Industries:	Art, design, technology, and marketing.
Example brands:	Apple, GoPro, Adobe, LEGO, Crayola, and Moleskine.

Table 5.2: Carl Jung's Brand Archetype #2: SAGE.

Dominant Traits:	Expertise. Influence. Wisdom. A thought leader. People see you as a credible and trustworthy source of information.
Desire:	To gain an understanding of the world through intelligence and analysis. To share valuable information that gains your audience deeper insight into topics.
Core Values:	Knowledge sharing, intelligence, and wisdom.
Drivers:	Self-reflection and a better understanding of others/the world.
Greatest Fear:	Ignorance. Being duped. To be misled.
Target Audience:	A loyal following of customers who rely on you and keep coming back for more knowledge.
Example Industries:	Education, news, and media industries.
Example brands:	Google, PBS, Universities, BBC, Mindvalley, TED.

Table 5.3: Carl Jung's Brand Archetype #3: CAREGIVER.

Dominant Traits:	Empathetic. Caring. Generous. Reassuring. Nurturing. Compassionate.
Desire:	Protecting and caring for others. Putting your customers first.
Core Values:	Service.
Drivers:	Empathy. Compassion. Generosity.
Greatest Fear:	Selfishness. Lies. Ingratitude.
Target Audience:	They respond to marketing messaging that includes emotional elements ... or shows empathy towards their lifestyle.
Example Industries:	Healthcare, nonprofit organizations, and baby products.
Example brands:	WWF, Pampers, Johnson & Johnson, Campbell's Soup, UNICEF, Toms Shoes, Pampers, Southwest Airlines.

Table 5.4: Carl Jung's Brand Archetype #4: INNOCENT.

Dominant Traits:	Having an incredibly positive outlook. Simple. Charming. Honest.
Desire:	To be sincere, pure, and unadulterated.
Core Values:	Safety.
Drivers:	Happiness, goodness, optimism, romance, and youth.
Greatest Fear:	To be punished for doing something bad or wrong.
Target Audience:	Customers value simple solutions, so avoid using confusing jargon.
Example Industries:	Organic or natural ingredients, such as in beauty, skincare, and food.
Example brands:	Dove, Coca-Cola, McDonald's, Nestle Pure Life, True Botanicals.

Table 5.5: Carl Jung's Brand Archetype #5: JESTER.

Dominant Traits:	Extremely charismatic. Optimist. Playful. Humorous. Likes to have fun and make some mischief. They don't take themselves too seriously and love to laugh.
Desire:	To bring joy to the world. To play, make jokes, have fun, and use humor to connect with the audience and encourage them to laugh along.
Core Values:	Pleasure.
Drivers:	To connect with others with full enjoyment. To bring pleasure to people wherever they are.
Greatest Fear:	Being bored or boring others.
Target Audience:	They want to have a good time and share memories. That will allow them to let go of stressful thoughts and come out of their shell to enjoy a little partying.
Example Industries:	Food, entertainment, and everyday home niches.
Example brands:	Dollar Shave Club, Doritos, Ben & Jerry's, M&Ms, Geico, Old Spice.

Table 5.6: Carl Jung's Brand Archetype #6: MAGICIAN.

Dominant Traits:	Mystical. A visionary and spiritual.
Desire:	To deliver transformative experiences that are almost spiritual and idealistic. To transport your audience to a utopian world where the only limit is their imagination.
Core Values:	Creativity and imagination.
Drivers:	Creating something special and making dreams come true.
Greatest Fear:	Unintended negative consequences.
Target Audience:	They want to try new and exciting things and live out their dreams at the same time. Take them on a mysterious journey and give them magical moments.
Example Industries:	Brands in the entertainment, hospitality, beauty, health, and relaxation industries ... including resorts and spas.
Example brands:	Disney, Red Bull, Tesla, Polaroid, Absolut.

Table 5.7: Carl Jung's Brand Archetype #7: RULER.

Dominant Traits:	Power. Dominance. Status. Success. An authoritative personality. Driven by a desire for power and control. A leader in your market. Wealthy, successful, and masculine ... traits associated with industry expertise.
Desire:	To influence others. To be the best of the very best.
Core Values:	Luxury, sophistication, perfection, and attention to detail.
Drivers:	To create order out of chaos.
Greatest Fear:	Chaos. Being overthrown.
Target Audience:	Customers are willing to pay a premium and won't settle for anything less.
Example Industries:	Luxury niches, from cars and hotels to jewelry, perfumes, and watches.
Example brands:	Rolex, Mercedes, Gillette, Microsoft, British Airways.

Table 5.8: Carl Jung's Brand Archetype #8: HERO.

Dominant Traits:	Brave. Persistent. Courageous. A source of inspiration. Honorable. Ambitious and embrace whatever challenges come their way.
Desire:	To leave a mark that proves their worth. To make the world a better place.
Core Values:	A strong drive to achieve mastery and motivate others to do the same.
Drivers:	To be as strong, courageous, and competent as possible. To inspire people to work harder.
Greatest Fear:	Weakness, vulnerability, or being a 'chicken'.
Target Audience:	Using the high-achievers your target audience identifies with as the public face of their brand. For example, Nike and Adidas use athletes like Roger Federer and Cristiano Ronaldo in their advertising campaigns.
Example Industries:	Sports, outdoor, and equipment manufacturers.
Example brands:	Nike, FedEx, Epicurious, BMW, Duracell.

Table 5.9: Brand Archetype #9: REGULAR GUY or EVERY WOMAN.

Dominant Traits:	Relatable, approachable, Dependable. Supportive, faithful, and down-to-earth.
Desire:	To connect with others and feel understood. To be affordable and inclusive and target the masses.
Core Values:	Seeking to connect and belong.
Drivers:	To develop ordinary solid virtues, be down to earth, and have empathy. To create a comfort zone for customers. They just want to blend in with the rest of society.
Greatest Fear:	To be left out. Standing out from the crowd. To have an elitist personality.
Target Audience:	Adopting a cost-leadership strategy is highly rewarding.
Example Industries:	Everyday brands, such as casual clothing, home decor and furniture, and food.
Example brands:	IKEA, Gap, Home Depot, AllRecipes, eBay.

Table 5.10: Carl Jung's Brand Archetype #10: REBEL or OUTLAW.

Dominant Traits:	A rebel at heart. Bold, disruptive, and questions authority. Breaks the rules, and dislikes conformity. Goes against societal norms just because she can.
Desire:	Freedom and revolution. To go against the established status quo. To leave a mark. To identify what isn't working, fix it, and get their audience to a better place.
Core Values:	Liberation.
Drivers:	Disruption. Rebellion.
Greatest Fear:	To be powerless or ineffective.
Target Audience:	Customers buy out of anger and because they like the thrill of anarchy. They express their unconventional personalities and aspirations. Your campaigns should go against stereotypical norms and routine.
Example Industries:	Statement jewelry, tattoos, and motorcycles tend to connect with a like-minded market segment.
Example brands:	Harley-Davidson, Diesel (jeans), Savage X Fenty, Virgin, Copy Posse.

Table 5.11: Carl Jung's Brand Archetype #11: EXPLORER.

Dominant Traits:	Pioneering, Exploration, Independence. Courageous, adventurous, and loving a challenge.
Desire:	To travel and visit new places and discover new people.
Core Values:	Discovery.
Drivers:	Travel, risk, discovery, and the thrill of new experiences.
Greatest Fear:	Boredom. Getting trapped. Conformity.
Target Audience:	They easily get bored. Dislike being confined in a safe and stable environment for too long. Love freedom. Always offer them a pathway to self-fulfillment. To change their surroundings & explore the outside world.
Example Industries:	Recreational activities and extreme sports.
Example brands:	Red Bull, Jeep, REI, The North Face, and Starbucks.

Table 5.12: Carl Jung's Brand Archetype #12: LOVER.

Dominant Traits:	Passionate. Affectionate. A true romantic. Values relationships above anything else. Finds strength in passion, inspires love, and commits to romance.
Desire:	Adoration. Intimacy. Sensual pleasure. Focus heavily on aesthetic appeal. And also advocate for all things beautiful and sensual.
Core Values:	Romance. Intimacy.
Drivers:	To be as attractive as possible, to be personal and passionate, and to make people want to know more about you.
Greatest Fear:	Being alone, unwanted, and unloved.
Target Audience:	Create brand messaging for your target audience that makes them feel loved.
Example Industries:	Luxury niches with products or services that offer indulgence in some way.
Example brands:	Chanel, Dior, Godiva, Victoria's Secret, Haagen Dazs.

Jennifer Aaker's 5 Brand Personality Frameworks

Jennifer Aaker ... a social psychologist, branding, and marketing expert ... coined the phrase 'brand personality framework' in 1997.

Her framework has since evolved to become the industry standard for brand personality.

She categorized brand personalities into five dimensions ... each with unique traits and strengths.

Ideally, your Aaker brand personality should fall into one of the categories below:

Table 5.13: Aaker's Brand Personality Framework #1: SINCERITY.

Dominant Traits:	Domestic. Kind. Approachable.
Desire:	To keep promises and meet expectations.
Primary Attributes:	Sincere.
Drivers:	Family, friendship, caregiving, gifting, service, honor, and generosity. Such a brand is wholesome, genuine, honest, warm, cheerful, and down-to-earth.
Target Audience:	Customers find brands like these to be credible and trustworthy.
Example Industries:	Food, hospitality, and safety brands.
Example brands:	Campbell's Soup, Hallmark, Oprah, Pampers, Allstate, Coca-Cola, and TOMS.

Table 5.14: Aaker's Brand Personality Framework #2: EXCITEMENT.

Dominant Traits:	Daring. Spirited. Imaginative. Cool. Unique. Contemporary. Anti-establishment.
Primary Attributes:	Funny. Playful. Attractive.
Desire:	To push limits and appeal to a younger demographic.
Drivers:	Creating hype and building enthusiasm among the audience.
Target Audience:	Attracted to energetic advertising that has a high-octane design. They prefer celebrity endorsements.
Example Industries:	Many brands that fall under this umbrella fall into several categories.
Example brands:	Virgin Atlantic, Monster Energy, Nike, MTV, T-Mobile, Mountain Dew, Vice, TikTok, and Axe.

Table 5.15: Aaker's Brand Personality Framework #3: COMPETENCE.

Dominant Traits:	Credible. Reliable. Responsible. Dependable. Trustworthy. Successful. Intelligent. Efficient.
Desire:	To be recognized as a qualified leader in your field.
Primary Attributes:	Inspires confidence.
Drivers:	Positioning in the market.
Target Audience:	Attracts customers by promising to get the job done. Consumer perceptions are based on how well a product or service performs.
Example Industries:	'Serious industry sectors' ... including banks, insurance companies, logistics firms, and life science brands.
Example brands:	Invitrogen, Chase, Verizon, UPS, Pfizer, Eppendorf, Volvo, and Microsoft.

Table 5.16: Aaker's Brand Personality #4: SOPHISTICATION.

Dominant Traits:	Luxury. Glamorous. Refined. High-class. Romantic. Charming.
Desire:	To position as upper-class.
Primary Attributes:	Poised. Polished. Classy. Elegant.
Drivers:	Status.
Target Audience:	Perceived by consumers as upper class.
Example Industries:	Sophistication brand personalities cut across categories. Found across many industries ... from fashion and accessories (watches and clothes) to cars, medical equipment, luxury hotels, food, and dining. Common in feminine brands or female-targeted brands.
Example brands:	Tiffany, Armani, Hermes, American Express, Apple, Mercedes, Nescafe, Grey Goose, and Patek Philippe.

Table 5.17: Aaker's Brand Personality Framework #5: RUGGEDNESS.

Dominant Traits:	Strong. Masculine. Thick-skinned. Outdoorsy. Tough. Western.
Desire:	Product performance.
Primary Attributes:	High-quality products that are built to last.
Drivers:	Durability.
Target Audience:	Rugged brands make customers feel powerful and remind them of nature.
Example Industries:	Rugged brands feature in construction and hardware, outdoor activities, sporting, and automotive.
Example brands:	Woodland, Harley Davidson, LL Bean, Otter Box, Milwaukee Tools, Land Rover, Levis, Jack Daniels, and REI.

Why Does Brand 'Voice' Matter?

Brand 'Voice' is essential for companies looking to succeed because it is a critical component of positioning. It gives your company a unique identity. And that is what your target audience connects with.

According to the *"Brand Loyalty Statistics"* study by Fundera.com, 89% of consumers stay loyal to brands that share their values.

So when it remains consistent and repeatable across all your content distribution channels ... from social media to your website, blog posts, emails, and advertisements ... your company remains identifiable to your buyers.

That way, it enhances your marketing efforts by differentiating you. It makes you stand apart from competitors. And makes it easy for your target audience to notice when you share content.

The Key Takeaways from Chapter 14:

1. Your brand 'Voice' or your brand's personality refers to the personification that puts a human face on your brand.

2. In 1919, Carl Jung ... a Swiss psychologist ... described the 12 brand personality archetypes.

3. In 1997, Jennifer Aaker coined the 5-dimensional brand personality framework. It classifies brands by how they display sincerity, excitement, competence, sophistication, or ruggedness.

4. Brand personality drives customer preference and enables you to differentiate your products. By identifying your brand's unique personality, you can make all your messaging decisions.

Coming Up In The Next Chapter ...

Pillar #2: Your Brand's 'Tone Of Voice'.

CHAPTER SIX

Pillar #2: Your Brand's 'Tone of Voice'

$\mathcal{Q}$uote

"Define what your brand
stands for, its core values,
and tone of voice, and then
communicate consistently in
those terms."

~ Simon Mainwaring ~
Branding Expert and Author of "We First".

Doug Kessler ... the co-founder and creative director at the B2B marketing agency Velocity Partners, says ... *"Traditional marketing talks at people. Content marketing talks with them."*

Take a moment and think about all the content you consistently share with your audience ... on your website, newsletters, emails, social media, advertising, videos, webinars, and customer service interactions ...

Do you understand your target audience's language preferences and style?

Your audience wants to read content that speaks to them ... not at them or past them. And your 'Tone of Voice' could make the difference between copy that works and copy that falls flat.

For example ...

When you combine direct second-person pronouns ... such as 'you' ... together with simple casual phrases, your 'Tone of Voice' can create a friendly and inviting tone

Similarly, when you use only third-person pronouns like 'he', 'she' or 'they' ... PLUS complex phrasing, and more technical terms and industry jargon ... by comparison, your 'Tone of Voice' adopts a more distant, formal tone.

Branding is about having a distinctive identity, and the way you communicate ... with your 'Tone of Voice' ... is a major part of that.

Brand 'Voice' Is The Driving Force Behind Your 'Tone of Voice'

The way you deliver content to your target audience is not only determined by the brand 'Voice', but also by your 'Tone of Voice'.

While your brand 'Voice' stays the same, your 'Tone of Voice' may vary slightly from time to time, depending on ...

1. *Your target audience:*
    If your target audience consists of more than one persona, you should tailor your messaging to speak to each one of them differently.

2. *The channels you use to distribute content:*
    Different media outlets call for different content formats.

3. *The content marketing goal or purchase decision-making stage you are targeting:*
   For instance, the goal of an article is to inform. The goal of a social media post is to engage and entertain.

Although there's a distinct difference between your brand's 'Voice' and 'Tone of Voice', they are interconnected and should collaborate in your messaging to strengthen your brand's appeal to consumers.

Consistency in 'Tone of Voice' Makes Your Messaging Memorable and Gives Your Brand a Distinctive Identity

Imagine the content you share with your target audience being a spoken conversation you have with your buyers.

And each time you post your content ... regardless of channel or platform ... you have a golden opportunity to think about how to apply your 'Tone of Voice' to connect with them.

How can you use phrases, sentence structure, and stylistic choices to set the mood?

'Tone of Voice' is an important aspect of your brand's personality that has to do with your messaging language.

It influences how people receive your message. It articulates your brand's unique personality and values. And it understands which words are best suited for usage under particular circumstances.

In other words ... it is central to your brand's identity.

And because the 'Tone of Voice' changes all the time ... depending on the content situation ... this sets the mood of that particular piece of content.

'Mood' is an emotional state that allows your audience to connect emotionally to your message.

So, if you apply it correctly in your messaging, it can become one of the tactics you use to activate your buyer's subconscious consumer triggers.

Thus, defining your 'Tone of Voice' ensures that your target audience will recognize consistency and that all your communication is standardized.

Consistency in brand messaging makes you memorable. And your audience is likely to remember your brand when making a purchase decision.

This impacts buyer decision-making more than any other marketing tactic.

Defining Your Brand's 'Tone of Voice'

Follow the steps below to define your brand's 'Tone of Voice' ...

Step #1: *Research To Understand Who Your Target Audience Is.*

Remember that your audience isn't made up solely of buyers. It may include everyone, from loyal customers to prospects finding you for the first time.

Defining your brand's 'Tone of Voice' starts with research to understand who your target audience is.

It would be best to use Google Analytics and other social media analytics to gather demographic information.

Use this information to create your buyer persona profiles.

Once you know who your target audience is, it becomes easier to choose the right language to reach them. And to figure out how to communicate with them using the type of messaging that will resonate most with them.

Step #2: *Highlight The Specific Goal Your Content Piece Aims To Achieve.*

Before you can decide what to write or how to say it, you need to define the purpose of your communication ... the specific goal your content piece aims to achieve.

This will make it easier to have tone guidelines that align with the goal of your content.

Step #3: *Identify The Core Values Your Brand Needs To Communicate.*

Your company's core values should inform the purpose of your communication. Determine the characteristics and guiding principles that are consistent with your company's culture.

This will help you find the right words to communicate in your message, so you can effectively connect with your customers.

Your core values will guide you in developing a 'tone of voice' that feels natural and authentic. Look at your competitors as you define your core values ... and determine what differentiates your brand and sets you apart from the crowd.

Step #4: *Choose Your 'Tone Of Voice' From The Nielsen Norman Dimensions*

According to Nielsen Norman Group, there are 4 dimensions of 'Tone of Voice' dimensions. That is ... humor, formality, respect, or enthusiasm. Each exists in a spectrum.

Choose one dimension as outlined in Table 6.1.

Then slide across the spectrum under each category to tailor the mood to your preferred taste.

Table 6.1: *The Nielsen Norman Group's 'Tone of Voice' dimensions.*

Dimension	Spectrum
1. Humor	Funny to serious: In this dimension, your 'Tone of Voice' can be cheerful, conservative, fun, funny, humorous, playful, serious, informative, quirky, or witty.
2. Formal	Formal to casual: In this dimension, your 'Tone of Voice' can be trustworthy, conversational, casual, formal, professional, frank, sympathetic, friendly, or smart.
3. Respectful	Respectful to irreverent: In this dimension, your 'Tone of Voice' can be caring, irreverent, provocative, edgy, respectful, unapologetic, sarcastic, snarky, or coarse.
4. Enthusiastic	Enthusiastic to matter-of-fact: In this dimension, your 'Tone of Voice' can be enthusiastic, matter-of-fact, passionate, upbeat, trendy, nostalgic, or romantic.

Since each dimension is a spectrum, you have to decide which position you want to pick for specific content types. And so, the possible combinations for your brand's 'Tone of Voice' are infinite.

Whichever tone works best for your message will depend on your brand's personality and target audience.

Always pick the combination that makes the most sense for your particular situation. And think about how your brand will implement that in all its communications.

Step #5: *Establish Clear 'Tone Of Voice' Guidelines.*

The next step is to audit your content and communication to establish clear 'Tone of Voice' guidelines. These will guide your team as they create content and general messaging.

Combine all voice characteristics into a single matrix with the 'Tone of Voice' dimensions in the rows. In the first column, you should briefly describe what each dimension means to your brand. Make sure to incorporate your identified core values into this.

Next, you will have a column for the DOs and another column for the DON'Ts. Share this with your content creation team, and ensure that they adhere to the guidelines in each communication your brand releases.

Step #6: *Incorporate Your 'Tone Of Voice' Into All Marketing Communication.*

Your target audience will greatly influence how your final communication looks.

For example, if you want to connect with millennials on social media, you could adopt a more fun and casual tone. You could also pepper your message with emojis to blend with the communication style of this audience.

However, a more mature audience might respond best to a highly authoritative tone ... with short sentences that go straight to the point.

For example ...

If you want the attention of senior scientists, the tone of your communication should be more professional.

You want to appear knowledgeable and provide thought leadership to a professional and more mature audience. You might also want to cultivate a following that will look to you for practical solutions and ideas.

Why Does Your Brand's 'Tone of Voice' Matter?

Here are some key reasons why it is important to develop your 'Tone of Voice'.

1. *Your target audience expects consistency in communication.*
   Defining your brand's personality and 'Tone of Voice' will go a long way toward standardizing all communication created by your company.

   In this way, your audience can identify you by how you communicate, which ensures gradual habituation.

   And as a reminder ... consistency in brand messaging impacts buyer decision-making more than any other marketing tactic.

   Maintaining a consistent 'Tone of Voice' across all of your messaging is critical to effective communication. It helps your audience recognize your brand, which enables quick association whenever they encounter your content.

2. *Identification of your brand by the public.*
   Unusual mood shifts in your messaging would make it difficult for your audience to understand your brand's behavior.

   But even in the face of situational changes, your overall 'Tone of Voice' should always be consistent with your brand's personality ... in every piece of content you share.

   Thus, a well-executed 'Tone of Voice' strategy will help your audience recognize your brand solely based on tone ... even if they don't see your logo or company name associated with the material you provide.

And when your brand consistently delivers your message over time, your message becomes clearer to your audience.

3. *Differentiation from competitors.*
To position yourself in a good spot, you need to think about the competition in your market and differentiate yourself.

Your brand's 'Tone of Voice' lets the public know how unique you are, which will help you stand out.

The 'Tone of Voice' helps to differentiate your business and communicates your values to your target audience.

The Key Takeaways from Chapter 15:

1. The 'Tone of Voice' is a central part of your brand's identity and influences how people perceive the messaging.

2. While your brand's personality stays the same, your 'Tone of Voice' changes all the time … depending on the situation.

3. Know why your 'Tone of Voice' enables you to adjust your language to your audience's preferences.

4. Defining your 'Tone of Voice' ensures that all your communication is standardized.

5. Brand consistency gives you brand recognition. It helps you build trust and loyalty. It evokes positive emotions about your brand. And it also helps you beat your competition.

Coming Up In The Next Chapter …

Pillar #3: The Message Map (Brand Messaging Framework)

CHAPTER SEVEN

Pillar #3: The Message Map (Brand Messaging Framework)

Quote

"The customer's
perception is your reality".

~ *Kate Zabriskie* ~
Business Trainer.

Web users are task-oriented. Each time they go online, they are only keen to find information that advances their goals. To fulfill their objectives and satisfy their wants, needs, and desires.

What they are not doing is spending time searching for your solutions.

In their *"2015 B2B Web Usability Report"*, KoMarketing revealed that people generally go online to search for their problems.

How can your business communicate effectively with them?

You need a structured and cohesive approach to messaging across different channels and platforms.

That will require establishing a clear and consistent messaging framework that aligns your content with your overall brand identity, values, and objectives.

A messaging framework can help you create coherent, impactful messages that resonate with your target audience.

It can also enable you to roll out effective communication across multiple channels, leading to better engagement, customer loyalty, and business growth.

What's In It For Me?

This is the only reason your prospects are looking at your content in the first place.

So, if your messaging focuses purely on your product and little else, your content will not have answered their most pressing question ... *What's In It For Me?* ... and will not appeal to your prospect's challenges, needs, or interests.

But if you cast your prospect as the star of your marketing message ... and present your product in a supporting role ... you will hook their attention.

It goes without saying that the main reason anyone would leave your site is if there's nothing in it for them.

So how do consumers perceive value?

In 2016, Harvard Business Review published "*30 Elements of Consumer Value: A Hierarchy ... Measuring—and delivering—what consumers really want*".

The authors ... Eric Almquist, John Senior, and Nicolas Bloch ... wanted to understand how consumers perceive value. So they first identified 4 levels of need that drive consumers: social impact, life-changing, emotional, and functional.

Then, they looked at each level of need and identified elements within each category that determined how consumers perceived value.

Lastly, they arranged these elements into a hierarchy, with the ones that have social impact at the top and those grouped as functional elements at the bottom (as outlined in Table 7.1).

What's important for you to note is that the 30 elements of value identified don't change. And that is ultimately what's going to be the most important thing to focus your messaging on as you plan your marketing content.

And for every product that you want to sell, you should ask yourself: What is the one core desire that you are going to channel?

Pick just one of the 30 elements of value for your entire promotional campaign.

Focus on it. Own it.

And every marketing piece that belongs to that specific campaign must speak to only that one element and not bring in any others.

You want to make sure that all of the messages you send about that one core desire build on each other.

When you do this for the whole customer journey, your messaging will be much more effective than if you just optimized each piece in isolation.

Table 7.1: The 30 Elements Of Perceived Consumer Value.

LEVELS OF NEED	THE SPECIFIC ELEMENTS OF CONSUMER VALUE
1. Social Impact	Self-Transcendence
2. Life-Changing	Provides Hope
	Self-Actualization
	Motivation
	Heirloom
	Affiliation / Belonging
3. Emotional	Reduces Anxiety
	Rewards Me
	Nostalgia
	Design / Aesthetics
	Badge Value
	Wellness
	Therapeutic Value
	Fun / Entertainment
	Attractiveness
	Provides Access
4. Functional	Saves Time
	Simplifies
	Makes Money
	Reduces Risk
	Organizes
	Integrates
	Connects
	Reduces Effort
	Avoids Hassles
	Reduces Cost
	Quality
	Variety
	Sensory Appeal
	Informs

But the secret to getting them hooked boils down to your ability to fulfill two things ...

1. To make a good first impression by clearly articulating your value proposition, and
2. To hold your buyer's attention long enough to successfully deliver your key business messages.

Let's Start With The Power Of A Good First Impression ...

In 2006, a study led by Princeton University professor Alexander Todorov ... published in Nature Human Behavior ... established that it takes just 0.05 seconds for people to make snap judgments.

He explained this in detail in his 2017 book entitled "*Face Value: The Irresistible Influence of First Impressions*".

In 2012, a Missouri University of Science and Technology study ... "*Eye-tracking studies: first impressions form quickly on the web*" ... found that it takes web users less than two-tenths of a second to form a first impression.

What does that mean for your content?

The audience you're trying to reach lives in a noisy world. That places great demands on their attention. And the only way to direct their attention to your content is to leave them with a good first impression.

But you don't have too much time for that either.

If your key message doesn't appeal to them within those precious few seconds ...

If they don't consider you to be likable, trustworthy, or competent ...

... they are going to bounce.

It then becomes difficult to win them back.

How come?

According to an article written in Psychology Today by Jack Schafer, Ph.D., "*Why Our Negative First Impressions Are So Powerful*" ... people find it difficult to move away from long-held beliefs. So once they form a negative opinion, they tend to hold steadfast to their original view.

This comes from the psychological principle of consistency.

For someone to change a negative first impression, they need to see new, compelling information. And then they would have to admit that they were initially wrong.

But admitting their error and adopting another position causes anxiety.

However, maintaining a false notion causes them less anxiety than doing the work to move away from their negative first impression. So they won't do it. They won't easily change their minds.

That's how critical a first impression is to your business.

You Have Little Time To Make Your Marketing Message Count

Once you go over the first impression, you need to hold onto your buyer's attention long enough to deliver your business messages ... and convince them to stay and consume more of your content.

But how much time do you really have to get them hooked?

According to a 2015 Consumer Insights study ... *"Attention Spans"* sponsored by Microsoft Canada ... on average, people focus on a task for just 8 seconds. They then lose concentration and switch their attention to something else.

So it comes down to ...

8 seconds!

That's about all the time you've got.

The more they rely on electronic devices to accomplish daily tasks, the less they can sustain their attention.

And so, whenever you share content, you need to quickly hook their attention by focusing your messaging on the only question that matters to them.

What's the main takeaway from this study?

When your buyers arrive on your website knowing little or nothing about your brand, you only have up to 8 seconds to capture their attention.

Ideally, for your message to impact your buyers, you want them to stick around a little longer than 8 seconds. This will give you enough time to fully convey your value proposition.

The most effective way to hook them is to make your 8-second message memorable.

How?

Steve Slaunwhite ... copywriting expert and award-winning marketing consultant, said ...

"Your business buyers are busy. Whether they are HR managers, IT directors, warehouse supervisors, or chiropractors. So for your marketing message to gain their interest, you need to hold their attention in the first few seconds of your communication. Otherwise, you'll lose them."

And Dr. Carmen Simon ... a cognitive neuroscientist who spent years researching what makes marketing content memorable, said ... *"If you send out multiple messages at the same time, your buyers won't hear you. You can't afford to send mixed messages. So you must stick with one message"*.

She cautions against cramming more than one message into your communication. She also cautions that if you do this, it will lower the likelihood that any message will stick.

She further states that memory is mandatory for business success. And your business can't survive unless you have customers. But you won't have customers unless you stay in their minds.

The Frolichstein-Stenitzer 'Message Map'

In the 1980s, Tripp Frolichstein and George Stenitzer developed the 'Message Map' as we know it today. They created it to work as an alignment framework that could be used to keep all marketing communication on message.

It has since evolved into the foundation upon which the content development process can be streamlined to deliver consistent messaging ... in all content and media briefings.

And by design, the 'Message Map' provides a useful structure for creating compelling communication. It does this by prioritizing key talking points in a hierarchical order.

This makes it easier for you to create messages that connect your audience to your brand ... in your web content, blogs, white papers, presentations, webinars, product videos, etc.

So, what does it look like?

The full-scale Frolichstein-Stenitzer 'Message Map' has 40 different elements. That is ...

- One core message ... also called the 'Home Base',
- 3 'Overarching Themes',
- 9 'Differentiating Proof Points' ... 3 for each 'Overarching Theme', and
- 27 'Supporting Examples' ... 3 for each 'Differentiating Proof Point'.

According to Dr. Carmen Simon ... a cognitive neuroscientist ... "*If you send out multiple messages at the same time, your buyers won't hear you. You can't afford to send mixed messages. So you must stick with one message*".

That's the purpose of the one core message ... your 'Home Base'.

It should tell your buyer what's in it for him right away.

But you need what Frolichstein and Stenitzer call a 7-second message to make a good first impression and hold your buyer's attention long enough to successfully deliver your key business messages.

The Frolichstein-Stenitzer 7-second message is designed to hook your buyer by communicating one core message, which is backed by 3 'Overarching Themes'.

It is structured to help your buyer discover his unconsidered needs or any other need he wasn't aware of already. So it should be positive, inspiring, and uplifting. It should also answer pertinent questions in your buyer's mind.

In addition, your 7-second message should be factual and speak your buyer's language ... instead of using industry jargon. It should also be consistent, and credible, and offer your buyer social proof.

How To Develop Your Brand's Messaging Framework

Creating a full 'Message Map' involves several key steps culminating in a framework that is summarized as a flow diagram on a single page.

The steps below explain how you can build yours …

STEP #1: *Start With Your Buyer Personas.*

> When writing your 'Message Map', your buyer personas are the best place to start, because that's the description of your target audience.
>
> Well-constructed personas will help your marketing team focus on your target audience. This will allow you to create messaging that's relevant to both your customers and prospects.
>
> In any communication, relevance is critical for credibility.

STEP #2: *Focus On One Core Message … Your 'Home Base'.*

> The Frolichstein-Stenitzer 'Message Map' centers on a 'Home Base'. This is your core message. The one main message that you will emphasize in all your communication.
>
> Its role is to engage your prospects emotionally by answering their question …
>
> What's in it for me?
>
> If you only focus on this one message, you will be able to reach 100% of your audience. But if you deliver two or more messages at the same time, it won't work.
>
> And so, the 'Home Base' is the core message that you must deliver in all your live, digital, and print media … consistently. Doing so will allow it to sink in with your audience.
>
> It's also a crucial starting point.
>
> But people need good reasons to believe your core message

because by itself, your 'Home Base' is insufficient to break through to people.

So back it up with 3 'Overarching Themes'.

STEP #3: *Identify 3 'Overarching Themes' That Will Give People Reasons To Believe Your Key Message.*

Why three?

Psychologists have found that detecting patterns is an important part of how humans learn and make decisions. A trio of words is the most memorable and impactful pattern.

The rule of three is a writing principle that explains why people grasp information through pattern recognition. Three is the smallest number needed for a pattern to be memorable.

Also, words grouped into threes are more appealing and easier to remember. That's why we have ...
... Three Wise Men
... Three Blind Mice
... Mind, Body, Spirit, etc.

If you want your prospects to remember anything, put it in a sequence of three.

With the 'Home base' and 3 'Overarching Themes', you now have the essence of your Frolichstein-Stenitzer 7-second message. You can quickly grab the attention of your audience and leave them hungry for more information.

STEP #4: *Back Up Each 'Overarching Theme' With 3 'Differentiating Proof Points'.*

Your 'Differentiating Proof Points' are the undeniable facts and figures about your product or brand. They are the elements of your brand or product that separate you from your competition.

These are the fundamental underpinnings of your product. They make your message far more powerful because your competitors can't claim them. They also allow you to expand your core message to make a compelling case. And provide the reason to believe your 'Overarching Themes'.

You need a total of 9 'Differentiating Proof Points' … 3 for each 'Overarching Theme'.

Choose them carefully because they will help you stand apart from your competition.

However, coming up with 'Differentiating Proof Points' is one of the most challenging parts of developing your 'Message Map'. You need to take an honest look at your offer and assess how it functionally solves your customers' pain points.

Steer clear of the obvious features and benefits. Allow yourself to dig deep and speak to the most compelling benefits that will give you leverage.

STEP #5: *Support Each 'Differentiating Proof Point' With 3 'Supporting Examples'.*

You need 27 'Supporting Examples' … 3 for each 'Differentiating Proof Point'.

These are your stories, anecdotes, quotes from customers, images, facts, or figures.

They work as social proof that provides reasons to believe your 3 'Overarching Themes', and help you create your full-scale 'Message Map'.

'Differentiating Proof Points' will earn you credibility.

STEP #6: *Testing Your 'Message Map'.*

George Stenitzer advises marketers to use a checklist to test their 'Message Map' before launch. This quality check ensures its relevance and resonance with your buyer personas.

The Primary Functions Of The Frolichstein-Stenitzer 'Message Map'

The primary functions of the Frolichstein-Stenitzer 'Message Map' are:

1. To create a layered system of communication that distills your brand's value down to its essential points.

2. To prioritize your buyer's needs by adapting your messaging to their personas.

Each content asset across your owned, earned, and paid media channels should communicate your core message. And each should work together to represent your brand's personality and 'Tone of Voice'.

But keeping your content on message can be a tough job to do because you always have to …

- create different content formats to deliver a multichannel experience ... across your owned, earned, and paid media channels,
- address multiple audiences, including consumers, partners, distributors, employees, influencers, and investors,
- create content for separate departments and geographic regions that might not even agree on what the message is, or
- work with different content creators and service providers ... such as bloggers, agencies, spokespersons, copywriters, and videographers.

Ideally, each product should have its own separate 'Message Map'.

You also want all your team members to feed your key messages into all your content and marketing channels. And through all departments of your company.

For your brand's messaging to be relevant to your buyer, it should convey the following 4 Cs …
- Clarity,
- Consistency,
- Continuity and
- Creativity.

The clarity of the message helps your audience remember your message. Clarity of purpose makes clear the action you want your buyer to take.

Consistency means that you reinforce the same message across all channels. It serves to ensure that all messages in your content assets are not contradictory.

You must deliver one message to your audience and convey the same message consistently over time. This is because consistency gives you credibility and strengthens your positioning.

It takes time for your message to sink in so that your buyers can remember it. Continuity ensures that you deliver messages that build on each other. This allows your content marketing campaign to be engaging.

And creativity helps you engage your buyer and keep him interested in your message. It also humanizes your brand, gives it character, and keeps your message real.

The cognitive elements of the human brain equate the 4 Cs with message relevance. Relevant messages are more credible. Credibility in business is highly associated with trust. But without trust, you will struggle to attract and retain customers.

While keeping your messaging consistent can be the tough part, doing so is key to your campaign's success.

When you create and disseminate your core messaging, you can align your sales and marketing teams around a common goal. This will help bolster collaboration and reduce intra-team friction.

A 'Message Map' Drives Content Ideas And Feeds Your Editorial Calendar

A 'Message Map' can be a driver of content ideas that you can plug into your editorial calendar. It can make an incredible difference in your content creation process.

It will guide and focus your content strategy. To coordinate the delivery of clear, targeted, and concise messages to your target audience. Especially if you share content on multiple platforms.

You want your sales, marketing, public relations, and customer service teams to tell the same company story ... consistently.

And so having a 'Message Map' can sharpen your message and get your entire team on the same page. It can also help you connect quickly with people in your market.

How?

According to BuzzSumo, if news media quote your company, the average sound bite is about 7 seconds, or 23 words.

The optimum length of a Facebook post is 15 words.

And that of a LinkedIn post is only 9 words.

The best length of a tweet is anything between 70 and 100 characters.

So always start by creating your Frolichstein-Stenitzer 7-second message. Some people call it their 7-second sound bite or elevator pitch.

And George Stenitzer says … *"If you can't relay your message in 7 seconds, you probably won't get to tell it at all".*

Let's look at an example of the 18-word message that George Stenitzer created for the Virgin Chicago Hotel.

And I quote …

"The Virgin Chicago Hotel delivers a great guest experience with a convenient location and comfortable rooms … and is ready for business. It's Virgin! It's fun!"

This is how George broke it down to its basic elements …

The Virgin Chicago Hotel delivers a great guest experience (the 'Home Base')

… with a convenient location ('Overarching Theme' #1),

… comfortable rooms, ready for business ('Overarching Theme' #2), and

… *"It's Virgin! It's fun!"* ('Overarching Theme' #3).

The idea here is to hook your target audience's attention with the first 7-second message so they can grant you their permission to see more. You can then expand your message to any length.

For example, if you want to expand your 'Message Map' to 2 minutes, all you need to add are the 3 'Overarching Themes' to your 'Home Base'.

If you want to expand your 'Message Map' to 20 minutes, you have to support your 'Home Base' with 3 'Overarching Themes' and support each 'Overarching Theme' with 3 'Differentiating Proof Points'.

You can take your message further by supporting each 'Differentiating Proof Point' with 3 'Supporting Examples'.

Imagine all the communication pieces you can create faster with a detailed structure like that.

You can now customize and fit your message to any content format or length ... including blogs, press releases, videos, and much more. You can then publish your content in any space ... digital, print, or live media ... while maintaining its clarity, consistency, continuity, and creativity.

The Key Takeaways from Chapter 16:

1. 'What's in it for me?' is the only message that matters to your buyer.

2. First impressions determine whether you can hold your buyer's attention to deliver your key business messages.

3. A good 'Message Map' feeds your editorial calendar and drives content ideas that boost your content creation process.

Coming Up In The Next Chapter ...

Pillar #4: Your editorial calendar.

CHAPTER EIGHT

Pillar #4: Your Editorial Calendar

Quote

"Give your audience enough variety that they won't get bored, with an emphasis on what they really want most".

~ Dustin W. Stout ~
Digital marketing consultant and Founder of SoVisual.co.

If you rely on content marketing to grow your business, you will find that you have to plan, produce, and schedule content to succeed in this effort. If you do not have a structure in place, you may find yourself buried under a mountain of missed deadlines, unedited content, and friction within your team.

Thus, staying organized is essential.

An Editorial Calendar

An editorial calendar (also known as a 'content calendar') is a visual workflow that allows you to plan when and where you will publish upcoming content on a daily, weekly, or monthly basis.

It often includes scheduling the creation of new content assets, mapping out distribution, collaborations, and revisions to existing content.

For many businesses, the use of an editorial calendar helps to ...

1. *1. Map out the execution of your content strategy.*

   If you want to successfully adopt a content strategy, the single most important tool you can use is a content calendar. It allows you to plan your editorial pieces ahead of time and guarantees that every content-related activity is actually completed. This will help you maintain order, post regularly, and promote your content efficiently.

   As it is for every other aspect of the creative process, planning your content should be given the same amount of attention.

   To establish a content calendar, you may make use of something as simple as spreadsheets.

   The amount of time it takes to construct a solid and complete content calendar, however, is totally dependent on what you are doing at the moment and how far in advance you are preparing.

2. *Stay on track with your content implementation plan.*

The process of making content consists of a million little steps. A reliable system keeps track of all those steps for each piece of content as it is processed. The use of automation can help your team collaborate more effectively and ensure timely content releases. So set up automated reminders and notifications to ensure you never miss another deadline.

3. *Streamline your content production workflow.*

Use customizable forms to keep track of all your content projects by gathering data in one location. This can facilitate strategic collaboration, monitor marketing performance, and identify opportunities for content repurposing.

4. *Maintain a consistent posting schedule.*

Of course, there is no hard-and-fast rule for how frequently you should post content. However, if you want to maintain an active presence before your target audience, it is recommended that you post frequently.

A content calendar allows teams to prioritize quality over quantity.

In addition, rather than publishing in a reactive or unplanned manner, planning will establish better consistency in terms of your brand's 'Voice' and style.

5. *Enhance your team's productivity.*

Editorial calendars can enhance your team's productivity and add clarity at every stage of your brand's content marketing journey when used thoughtfully.

6. *Set up strategic collaboration with your team and external partners.*

It makes it easier for you to communicate not just with members of your team but also with partners outside of your organization.

The Editorial Calendar Is A Planning Tool

An editorial calendar is an essential tool for planning and organizing content production. It provides a structured framework that ensures a consistent flow of high-quality content according to predetermined goals and audience preferences.

It provides a comprehensive overview of upcoming topics, publication dates, and responsible team members, allowing you to align your content creation with your marketing goals to maintain a consistent brand voice.

Additionally, it can facilitate collaboration between different stakeholders and the repurposing of content across various platforms. Maximizing its reach and impact. And ensuring the timely delivery of high-quality content to your audience.

Thus, it can help you plan, organize, and execute your content strategy efficiently. It can also help you manage your content pipeline, track progress, and ensure that your content strategy is aligned with your overall marketing goals.

Coming Up In The Next Chapter ...

Pillar #5: Content Distribution (Owned, Earned, and Paid Media)

CHAPTER NINE

Pillar #5: Content Distribution (Owned, Earned, and Paid Media)

$$\mathcal{Q}uote$$

"Before you create any more
'great content', figure out
how you are going to market
it first".

*~ **Joe Pulizzi & Newt Barrett** ~*
Co-authors of "Get Content Get Customers: Turn
Prospects into Buyers with Content Marketing".

Great content is practically useless if your audience doesn't know it exists. And if no one interacts with the content you create, you're just wasting your time, energy, and resources by cluttering an already crowded internet.

Here's why …

In 2019, a study by Backlinko.com found that 94% of online content doesn't get any traffic or backlinks from Google.

Not even a single visitor? Wow!

While there are many SEO issues responsible for low traffic, what can you do to place your content in the 6% sweet spot that attracts attention?

Picking the right platform to distribute your content is as important as knowing the types of content that resonate with your buyers.

According to Hubspot … *"Content distribution is the process of sharing, publishing, and promoting your content. It's how you provide your content to your audience for their consumption through various channels and media formats"*.

Content distribution is an essential part of your content strategy and is as critical as the quality of the writing itself. It improves the reach of your content. It also gets you more social shares and drives traffic to your website.

As a rule of thumb, your distribution plan should fit into your business model and support your marketing goals. Your buyer personas should help you know which platforms your prospects primarily use.

You have three overarching types of distribution channels to choose from:

- Your 'owned' channels,
- 'Earned' or 'shared' channels, and
- 'Paid' content distribution channels.

Leveraging owned, earned, and paid distribution channels will keep you pumping content to the right places. However, your choice of content distribution channels will depend on who you want to reach and how much money you have.

Let's Start By Looking At Your 'Owned' Content Distribution Channels …

As the name suggests, you own these media channels. They are under your jurisdiction and ownership. They are yours and yours alone.

When you use your 'owned' distribution outlets, you have absolute control and say over what you post, how to present the content, and when you share it.

And so, ideally, you want your owned media channels to be the main outlets through which you distribute your digital content.

But you must work to drive traffic to your content. You want your target audience to visit your 'owned' spaces regularly.

'Owned' content distribution channels include:

Channel #1: *Your Website.*

> Your website is your virtual identity card. Your online real estate.
>
> It should communicate your brand's promise and value proposition. It should differentiate you from the competition and help you meet your marketing goals.
>
> If you follow the best SEO practices, your site will get more organic traffic from Google search results. It will also position your site for greater online visibility.
>
> But if you want to engage your visitors, you must use persuasive, customer-focused copy. And if you want to encourage them to respond to your call to action, you must add lead-generation elements to your webpages.
>
> Having a website makes it very easy for your buyers to find you, discover what you're about, and answer a bunch of questions they have. But one of the main reasons you should have a website is to increase your brand's credibility.

Channel #2: *Your Blog.*

A blog, which is short for 'weblog', is a section of your website where you can share personal commentary or business content.

It allows you to have informal diary-style text entries ... known as posts ... where you share information or opinions on topics relevant to your audience.

These posts appear in reverse chronological order, with the most recent at the top.

You can optimize your blog with keywords that make it SEO-compliant for search engines.

Blogs are ideal for all types of businesses. They make people more aware of your brand, bring in new leads, and help build loyalty and trust. \

Channel #3: *Your Email Newsletters (eNewsletters).*

Email is ideal for all types of businesses.

Email marketing offers you a channel through which you can share information with your subscribers. These are people who are already familiar with your brand.

eNewsletters give you one of the best methods to build relationships with your subscribers. They can also help you tell your readers about new products, upcoming events, or product promotions.

And to engage your audience, you can enrich your eNewsletters with videos, images, GIFs, and infographics.

Channel #4: *Your Video Channels (YouTube).*

YouTube is the largest video-sharing platform. It allows all types of businesses to create and publish video content. Depending on the marketing goals of your brand, you can create either educational or entertaining videos.

And since Google owns YouTube, you can use pay-per-click (PPC) ads from your AdSense account to promote your content to a wider audience.

You can always link your video content to your website to keep your users on your webpages for longer.

Most people find watching videos more enjoyable than reading text. Also, videos are more effective at helping people retain information.

Channel #5: *Your Podcasts.*

A podcast is a collection of prerecorded audio content that is distributed regularly online in the form of episodes.

Podcasts offer you the opportunity to repurpose your content. For example, you record an interview with an expert, then repurpose it on your blog or use the script to make a YouTube video.

Not only can you invite experts to your podcast, but you can also be a guest on others to reach a new audience.

All types of businesses can use this platform. And you can turn interesting topics into discussions with thought leaders, experts, and other guest speakers.

Channel #6: *Your Mobile Apps.*

An app ... short for 'application' ... is a type of software that runs on a mobile electronic device ... such as a tablet or a smartphone.

Most web-based apps need internet access to be used.

You can integrate your app content with social media to improve the user experience. The important thing is to focus on creating meaningful and distinctive content that will engage your users.

Channel #7: *Your eBooks.*

An eBook is a long-form piece of content that you can use to offer your target audience in-depth expertise on a topic.

If well written, your eBook should provide insightful information. And become an effective instrument to reach a wider audience.

eBooks are ideal for use as downloadable lead magnets by all types of businesses.

Channel #8: *Your Social Media Profile.*

Social media are interactive platforms that offer virtual networks for the sharing of content.

LinkedIn is a business channel ideal for all types of businesses. It's an informal virtual space where professionals meet and follow industry trends. Most of the content shared on LinkedIn is usually informative rather than entertaining.

Facebook is the biggest social media platform. It is ideal for all types of businesses. With over 2.7 billion active users, it offers more opportunities and tools that can enable you to boost your content and reach a larger audience. You can create common interest groups to share relevant information.

Twitter (also known as X) is a microblogging site that is ideal for all types of businesses. It has become popular for its ability to drive the news cycle and facilitate quick customer service. On this platform, hashtags allow you to keep up with the latest trends that interest you. You can also upload and share short videos and photos.

Instagram is a great platform for sharing photos and videos that are aesthetically pleasing. Any business can use it to showcase its products, services, or brand culture. And it has a paid option available to promote content from your profile.

Channel #9: *Your Webinar.*

> A webinar is an online educational presentation that can be pre-recorded or held live in real time for a more interactive format.

> Participants can join you from anywhere in the world.

> With the pre-recorded version, you can let people sign up whenever they want and give them access whenever it's convenient for them.

> Webinars are ideal for all types of businesses.

'Earned' or 'Shared' Content Distribution Channels

When third parties distribute your content for free to their followers ... or create content about you ... you get 'Earned' or 'Shared' content.

The advantage of 'Earned' or 'Shared' content is that it works as social proof.

The downside of this kind of content is that it ultimately falls under the control of a third party. And their decisions can change at a moment's notice.

'Earned' or 'Shared' content distribution channels include:

Channel #10: *Press Coverage.*

> Press coverage gives you free publicity. This includes getting news outlets to write about your brand when it does something newsworthy.

> Typically, a journalist will find your information interesting enough to write a story about it.

> While it may happen organically, it can help if you reach out with proactive public relations and put yourself on people's radars.

> Getting press coverage is a great way to raise awareness. It can also have a snowball effect, whereby the initial press coverage begets

more press.

Businesses with a lot of press coverage are easier to find, which makes their stories more likely to appear in other outlets.

Channel #11: *Guest Posting and Article Contributions.*

Guest posting involves contributing original, high-quality content as a guest on a blog or in a reputable publication.

It helps you reach a wider audience, build trust, and build your online presence.

It's a great way to establish thought leadership and boost your credibility.

Channel #12: *Retweets, Shares, And Reposts.*

Retweets, shares, and reposts account for a large part of 'Shared' content.

They are important components of your social media strategy that can help spread your message and expand your reach to new audiences.

Shares and retweets are excellent at getting your message to go viral. In the age of social media, a viral campaign is a low-cost method to distribute your content. Going viral means your content resonates so much that many people spread it to their followers for free.

Being in tune with your industry ensures that you're up-to-date when something important breaks. And this helps you take advantage of opportunities as they arise.

Channel #13: *Customer Reviews And Star Ratings.*

A customer review is a form of customer feedback or comment made by a customer who has purchased and used a product or service.

A star rating is a form of consumer review that grades quality. Whereas a 5-star rating stands for the best quality, a 1-star rating stands for poor quality.

Customer reviews and star ratings help to build social proof. Social proof is a phenomenon where people want to buy a product based on the assurance of others.

While reviews happen organically, you can ask your paid customers to submit theirs and leverage their input to get more business.

When you respond to less-than-favorable comments, you come off as trustworthy, which will improve your image.

Channel #14: *Speaking Or Presenting At Events.*

Let's say you have to speak at a conference ...

From the minute you confirm your appearance until weeks after you get back from the event, you can use content to inform your audience.

For example ...

Before the speaking engagement, you can create a blog post about the event that lets your audience know you'll be there. You can follow up by scheduling a social promotion that links to the session to get your network interested and alerted.

You then send out an email to your leads and clients to let them know the schedule of your speaking event.

During the speaking engagement, you can live tweet. You can also bring brochures and one-sheet documents to distribute to session attendees.

After the speaking engagement, have an outreach plan in mind. Keep track of all the business cards you receive.

'Paid' Content Distribution Channels

In 'paid' content distribution channels, you must explicitly pay before your content goes out.

'Paid' content distribution channels include:

Channel #15: *Cost-Per-Click (CPC) Model.*

Payment may be made in a variety of ways, although it frequently follows a cost-per-click (CPC) model.

Under this arrangement, the advertiser only pays when someone views or clicks on their advertisement.

The advantage of a CPC model is that it allows you to factor in bidding strategies relative to your budget size and target keywords.

Channel #16: *Sponsored Content.*

Sponsored content is an advertisement where you pay an individual to share your content on their platform.

It works best when you hire someone whose brand already appeals to your audience and buyer personas.

As a result, sponsored content feels natural when it aligns well with your brand. It feels less invasive or disruptive to the target audience.

You can use sponsored content in many ways ... as photographs, videos, podcasts, social media posts, or any other influencer content.

Channel #17: *Influencer Marketing.*

For influencer marketing to work, you need to hire the best content creators in your field. They will help you create brand awareness, draw in traffic, and improve conversions among your shared audience.

It is most effective when it taps into strategies like word-of-mouth marketing and social proof. For most buyers, this will feel more trustworthy and believable than the marketing they receive when a company does it directly.

Channel #18: *Press Releases.*

If your company has some extra cash, you may consider hiring a public relations agency. PR firms can give you access to a variety of content distribution options.

They have a wide reach in content marketing channels, from newspapers to partner websites. You may use their skills to get things started and reach a broader audience.

You may also target particular audiences with the news and events that you publish and promote through the use of PR Newswire, which is a paid press release distribution network.

But if you don't want to spend money, you don't have to hire a PR firm to take care of your needs. You can use one of the open-source services available online.

PRlog is one of them. It's a free service that provides a wide range of news distribution options without charging a fee.

You may publish information by location or industry, and you can include video press releases, links, and other features.

Keep in mind that press releases work great ...

- When you announce the release of a new product or service.
- When your company is hosting a major event or function.
- When you change something about your brand (new website, name, logo, slogan, etc.).
- When you donate to a good cause or charity.
- When you host a webinar or publish an eBook.
- When you launch a new marketing campaign.

CASE STUDY: How A Leading Biotech Brand Distributes Content

Thermo Fisher Scientific is a leading Biotech brand. They manufacture scientific instruments, reagents, consumables, and software.

Their main clients include healthcare facilities and laboratories in research and academic institutions. These are organizations in the biotechnology and pharmaceutical sectors.

With a large budget, Thermo Fisher Scientific creates different content pieces. Then they distribute them across several social media platforms.

They often upload a variety of photographs, videos, industry reports, and other content on Facebook and LinkedIn.

On Twitter, they describe their target audience in their profile.

Their learning resources webpage ... which would be the equivalent of a blog ... is also full of new content assets in different formats.

One would assume that a company this size ... with revenues of $17 billion and 50,000 employees in 50 countries ... wouldn't need to promote its content.

One may argue that they don't even need to have a content marketing plan to begin with.

Wrong!

Not only do they have a content strategy, but they also create different types of content and distribute it to various owned and paid channels.

If content creation and distribution are important to them, then they are certainly important to your company too.

The Key Takeaways from Chapter 18:

1. Content distribution involves using media outlets to share, publish, or promote content to an audience.

2. 'Owned' content distribution channels are under your jurisdiction and ownership.

3. When third parties distribute your content for free to their followers ... or create content about you ... then you call this kind of content 'Earned' or 'Shared'.

Coming Up In The Next Chapter ...

Pillar #6: Performance Metrics For Tracking A Content Strategy

CHAPTER TEN

Pillar #6: Performance Metrics For Tracking A Content Strategy

$$\mathcal{Q}uote$$

"Few managers appreciate the range of metrics by which they can evaluate marketing strategies and dynamics. Fewer still understand the pros, cons, and nuances of each".

~ Paul W. Farris ~
Marketing Metrics: The Definitive Guide
to Measuring Marketing Performance.

Every content marketer expects their campaign to generate results. But merely setting up a campaign is not enough to ensure its success. How can you know if your content campaign is actually working?

The marketing consultant ... Ian Brodie, said ... *"Without the right marketing metrics, you are shooting in the dark. The only way to know if things are working for you or not, are those metrics".*

If you fail to stay on top of your campaign numbers, you'll never get a holistic view of when you have opportunities or threats.

So, what do you need to do?

Industry experts recommend that the first step you must take is to be clear about the business goals of your campaign (which were covered in Chapter 3).

Here's why ...

Jay Baer ... the author of Hug Your Haters, said ... *"The goal of content marketing is not to be good at content. It is to be good at business".*

And Stoney deGeyter ... the Founder and CEO of Pole Position Marketing Agency, said ... *"Without goals, you will have no way to know whether what you're doing works or not".*

So once you have your goals set, what do you need to do next?

Stoney deGeyter went on to say ... *"Each goal will have different measurements. You won't necessarily hit them right away, but with time, you should start seeing the needle move".*

This is what campaign tracking is all about ... in a nutshell.

But there's more ...

Andrea Fryrear ... the chief content officer at Fox Content, said ... *"Above all, don't start releasing content until you know what you want to measure, how to get that data, and what you plan to do with it once you've got it."*

Because if you don't measure your content marketing efforts, you won't know what's working and what's not working.

Campaign monitoring allows you to observe, understand, and track target audience behavior. So you can determine which tactics successfully get them to respond more to your call to action.

It also allows you to track the performance of every content asset you distribute against the business goals you've established.

This will enable you to gauge the effectiveness of your campaign and determine if you should continue with the marketing technique you are using … or stop it.

Ultimately, the data that you collect from your campaigns may help you rethink your goals and formulate new strategies for the future.

But remember, always keep records of the metrics you monitor. Because over time, you may occasionally need to adjust your strategy as you track your progress.

And you must revisit your initial expectations at the end of every campaign to establish what worked, what didn't, and why not.

However, since every goal will need different indicators, metrics, or benchmarks against which you will measure your results … if you are like most marketers … you will probably struggle with identifying the right things to measure and how to determine the outcome of your campaign.

That's what we are going to cover in this chapter.

What Performance Metrics Should You Track To Monitor Your Content Campaign?

Since content marketing is a big-picture strategy … whose success hinges on a well-organized marketing lifecycle, from planning to content distribution … knowing exactly which numbers to measure starts with the goals of your content marketing strategy.

But the business goal of your content marketing strategy should be the primary guide that helps you identify the crucial metrics you need to monitor.

For example …

If your goal is to increase brand awareness, you should monitor website views and mentions, track social media followers, and track the number of leads you generate.

And if your goal is to generate more sales revenue, you should focus on increasing conversion rates or your average order values.

So keep an eye on the most important metrics and track them consistently over time to gain valuable insights that will help you identify trends.

As a result, you will be in a good position to tweak your strategy and make the necessary adjustments.

The metrics you should watch are generally categorized into 5 groups. That is ...

1. Website content performance metrics,
2. Social media content performance metrics,
3. User engagement and behavior metrics,
4. Search engine optimization (SEO) metrics, and
5. Metrics for tracking the business results of your content campaign.

Let's now look at how each category is broken down further into performance scores from which you can select the most relevant metric to track your content strategy.

1. Website Content Performance Metrics

Website content plays a crucial role as the face of your brand, conveying important information to your target audience and guiding them toward desired actions.

Tracking specific metrics related to your website can give you valuable insights into the functionality of your web content and guide you to make data-driven decisions that enhance the user experience.

Google Analytics remains one of the most powerful tools you have to track the right metrics about your website and target audience.

Table 10.1 outlines different metrics that can inform specific performance attributes about your site.

Table 10.1: Website content performance metrics.

Performance Score	Remarks
Traffic Sources:	*What It Is:* This is a report that reveals where your web traffic is coming from. *Why It Matters:* Knowing all the places from where your traffic originates can help you improve your targeting. *How to Use It:* Knowing where your target audience spends time should inform your content distribution choices.
Bounce Rates:	*What It Is:* The proportion of website visitors who only visit one page and leave (i.e., 'bounce') without going to another page. *Why It Matters:* A high bounce rate suggests you're attracting the wrong visitors, who find nothing on your site for them. *How to Use It:* Revisit your keywords to better target your prospects, and make the purpose of your webpage immediately clear.
Click-Through Rate (CTR):	*What It Is:* The percentage of people who are exposed to a webpage, search link, ad, or email ... and click on it. *Why It Matters:* There is a strong correlation between Google page rank and click-through rate (CTR). *How to Use It:* Tailor the title of your page to the user's Google search intent to improve how your page shows up in search results.
New Website Visitors:	*What It Is:* The people who arrive on your website for the very first time. *Why It Matters:* New site visitors mean you're increasing your brand's exposure, and people are finding your site, which is a good thing. *How to Use It:* Align your web content, landing pages, and user experience to answer your buyer persona's questions.
Rate Of Returning Web Visitors:	*What It Is:* The percentage of visitors to your website who return. *Why It Matters:* Monitoring the rate of repeat visits provides insight into the extent to which your audience engages with your content. *How to Use It:* Returning visitors have a higher likelihood of conversion.

Number Of Pages Viewed Per Visit:	What It Is: How many Web pages a particular visitor views on a single website per session. Why It Matters: It provides information about the capacity of your content to move page visitors farther down your conversion funnel. How to Use It: Use videos, surveys, tools, etc. to engage with them, make your site navigation simple, and page layout clear.
Average Time Spent On Site:	What It Is: The average time on site metric informs you about how engaging your site is to your visitors. Why It Matters: It can help pinpoint specific issues you must address, such as poor navigation or a lack of content. How to Use It: Ensure your site is mobile-friendly. Verify that the session duration is consistent with the information volume on the page.
Page Speed:	What It Is: Page speed refers to the time it takes to fully display the content on a specific webpage. Why It Matters: Google's algorithm favors websites that load faster. How to Use It: Reducing the page load time will lead to a better user experience, higher search rankings, and more organic traffic.

2. *Social Media Content Performance Metrics*

Many marketers post content on social media platforms. But what most don't realize is that every social platform has native analytics tools.

Social media analytics can be a good starting point for generating data about your target audience's demographics and interests. It can help you refine your buyer personas and guide you to target a new lookalike audience.

Table 10.2 outlines different metrics that can inform specific performance attributes about how your social media content is giving you visibility.

Table 10.2: Social media content performance metrics.

Performance Score	Remarks
Impressions:	*What It Is:* Impressions record how many times your content shows up on social media when users go through their feed page. *Why It Matters:* This gives you a clear sense of whether you're reaching your audience. *How to Use It:* As rankings improve, impressions will increase.
Reach:	*What It Is:* When you think about reach, you should picture sharing content to influence as many people in your target audience as possible. *Why It Matters:* Social media can help you reach a new pool of potential buyers who know nothing about your brand but might like what you offer. *How to Use It:* Research your target audience's social media preferences to find out where they hang out.
Influence:	*What It Is:* Who's talking about your brand, and what kind of impact have their interactions with it had? *Why It Matters:* Influence helps you decide who to reach with your campaign. *How to Use It:* Measure your online social capital and the ability to influence others.

3. *User Behavior And Engagement Metrics*

In a low-attention digital world, content engagement gives insights into what resonates with users … and what doesn't. And so, beyond the visibility you can get from social media, you also want your target audience to engage and interact with your brand.

Behavior metrics help you see how your content aligns with the interests of your audience. And the frequency with which your audience engages with your content is a prime indicator of the value they derive from it.

Table 10.3 outlines different user behavior and engagement metrics that provide insights into how well your target audience is engaging with and interacting with your brand.

Table 10.3: User behavior and engagement metrics.

Performance Score	Remarks
Likes or Dislikes:	*What It Is*: Likes and dislikes of social media content allow you to gauge viewer sentiments about posts. *Why It Matters*: Likes tell you what works. Dislikes communicate displeasure. *How to Use It*: You should celebrate dislikes because they reveal what your audience prefers not to see.
Shares and Retweets:	*What It Is*: When your social media viewers pass on your content to their audiences. *Why It Matters*: Shares and retweets can make your message go viral. This presents your content to potential leads that you wouldn't otherwise reach. *How to Use It*: Tune into your industry to ensure that when something important breaks, you can take advantage of the opportunity to go viral.
Comments:	*What It Is*: The short-form messages your audience leaves behind in response to your content. *Why It Matters*: Commenting allows your audience to express their thoughts and ideas. *How to Use It*: Responding to comments is a one-on-one way to nurture and serve customers.
Follows:	*What It Is*: A social media follower is a user who chooses to see all of your posts in their news feed. *Why It Matters*: A large social media following could make any content you post go viral. *How to Use It*: Build a long list of followers.
Number of Subscribers:	*What It Is*: The people who connect their social media profiles to yours. *Why It Matters*: Having engaged subscribers is more important than having many followers. *How to Use It*: Look at your subscriber growth rate over time. A consistent growth rate will help you justify the dedication you put in.
The Number of Video Views:	*What It Is*: A video played in a user's feed for 30 seconds on TikTok, 3 seconds on YouTube or Facebook, and 2 seconds on Instagram or Twitter. *Why It Matters*: Knowing how different platforms track views can save you time and money and help your ads reach their target audience. *How to Use It*: No two platforms are alike. Rethink or improve your video strategy to make the views count.

Video Watch Time:	What It Is: The total amount of time someone spent watching your video. Why It Matters: Watch Time is an important metric that feeds into the search and discovery algorithms. How to Use It: The strategies that boost audience retention, like creating long, engaging videos, can help you get more watch time.
Customer Reviews & Star Ratings:	What It Is: A customer review is a type of online feedback that a customer who has purchased a product or service provides. Why It Matters: 90% of consumers trust reviews and ratings as personal recommendations so they can make or break your brand's reputation. How to Use It: Use it as social proof. Customer reviews carry a lot of weight in the decision-making process.
Email Open Rates:	What It Is: The percentage of recipients of a marketing email campaign who click to open it. Why It Matters: It shows how engaged your email recipients are with your email content. How to Use It: Open rates are useful for tracking the overall performance of your email campaigns.

4. Search Engine Optimization (SEO) Metrics

When a web user submits a search query on Google, the algorithm will return a list of the most relevant results. How high your website appears on that list depends on the page title, meta description, and keywords.

If your prospect's search query matches the keywords in your content, your site will rank highly in the Google search results. But Google has a long history of always updating its algorithm.

One way to keep up with the constant changes is to regularly track your SEO metrics.

Always use the analytics platform to check your search engine rankings for your target keywords and web traffic. Monitoring these metrics will ensure that your website's content remains optimized. This will help support your content marketing goals.

Table 10.4 outlines search engine optimization (SEO) metrics that provide data, which your marketing team can use to devise new strategies that will improve your tactics.

Table 10.4: Search engine optimization (SEO) metrics.

Performance Score	Remarks
Organic Traffic:	*What It Is:* Visitors who land on your website from search engines ... and not paid ads. *Why It Matters:* Content that attracts organic traffic matches the search intent of high-quality leads. *How to Use It:* You have a high chance of converting high-quality leads. Nurture them to move them along your sales funnel.
Backlinks:	*What It Is:* Inbound links on other websites that are not your own but go back to a page on your website. *Why It Matters:* Backlinks symbolize a vote of confidence by the online community about your website content. *How to Use It:* Backlinks are an essential part of SEO. New links from domains that have never linked to your site have more impact.
Keyword Searches:	*What It Is:* The language your target audience types into a search engine query when they look for your products, services, or content. *Why It Matters:* Keyword optimization can boost your traffic and connect you to your most likely target audience. *How to Use It:* Use tools such as Google Keywords to examine the keywords that are driving visits and, more importantly, conversions.
Keyword Ranking:	*What It Is:* When you talk about keyword rankings, you're talking about where your page is on the search results page for a particular search query. *Why It Matters:* Rankings provide an overview of your organic search market share and help you benchmark the progress of your SEO strategy. *How to Use It:* Focus on both branded and non-branded words and phrases that people type into search engines to find what they're looking for.
Organic Visibility (aka Organic Market Share):	*What It Is:* A score that measures how much search volume and ranking position your site gets compared to the total number of available clicks. *Why It Matters:* Provides you with a snapshot of your site's SEO performance. *How to Use It:* A score that demonstrates how well you target and engage your potential consumers.

Domain Authority:	*What It Is:* It's a rating used to calculate the overall strength of your URL in search engines. *Why It Matters:* Sites with higher domain authority perform better in search rankings than those with lower authority. *How to Use It:* This rating may be used to compare websites or monitor a website's 'ranking strength' over time.
On-Page Optimization Scores:	*What It Is:* The process of using keywords to optimize the contents of a webpage … both for users and search engines. *Why It Matters:* On-page optimization helps you rank higher in organic search results. *How to Use It:* The on-page SEO results can help you make adjustments to improve your search rankings and boost traffic to your site.
Text Readability SEO Metrics:	*What It Is:* A score that measures how easy it is for someone to read and understand the text messages of your content. *Why It Matters:* A highly readable website is more likely to convert visitors because simple, clear language is more persuasive. *How to Use It:* Use actionable content with clear takeaways. Also, use the active voice and transition words in shorter sentences, paragraphs, and sections.

5. *Metrics for Tracking The Business Results Of Your Content Campaign*

Joe Pulizzi … the founder of the Content Marketing Institute, said … *"Businesses only care about three things … sales, savings, and sunshine".*

He lumps together customer loyalty, retention, cross-sales, and advocacy into the sunshine phase. But cautions that you can never know if you have sunshine unless you quantify the gains.

Table 10.5 outlines different metrics that provide data for measuring the business success of your content marketing campaign.

Table 10.5: Metrics for tracking the business results of a content campaign.

Performance Score	Remarks
New Leads Generated:	*What It Is:* People who've engaged with your marketing team's efforts for the first time and shown interest in your brand's products or services. *Why It Matters:* Leads are the lifeblood of every business. Generating new leads is a key part of growing a successful business. *How to Use It:* You have to follow up with the new leads and nurture them. Warm them up and nudge them toward a possible sale.
Lead Conversion Rate:	*What It Is:* The percentage of visitors to your website who are captured as leads. *Why It Matters:* It helps you measure the effectiveness of your marketing strategy. *How to Use It:* It indicates how successful your marketing is at attracting the right audience. And how well your website can turn visitors into leads.
Cost Per Acquisition (CPA):	*What It Is:* It measures the aggregate cost of acquiring a single paying customer from a campaign. *Why It Matters:* It informs you how much of your revenue is going towards content marketing campaigns. *How to Use It:* It can help you optimize your return on investment.
Customer Lifetime Value:	*What It Is:* The total worth of your buyer to your business over the entire duration of your relationship with him. *Why It Matters:* The higher it is, the bigger your profits. *How to Use It:* It can predict how much revenue a customer can bring to your business.
Return On Investment (ROI):	*What It Is:* A widely used financial metric for measuring the probability of an investment (in this case, content marketing). *Why It Matters:* It establishes the amount of profit an expenditure generates. *How to Use It:* It allows you to make financial decisions that will help you grow your business.

The Key Takeaways from Chapter 19:

1. Content marketing is a big-picture strategy whose success hinges on a well-organized lifecycle ... from planning to content distribution.

2. Campaign monitoring is crucial for demonstrating the effectiveness of your content marketing strategy.

3. Content engagement metrics can give you invaluable insights into what resonates with your users.

4. Monitoring SEO metrics ensures that your site remains optimized to support your content goals.

Coming Up In The Next Chapter ...

PART 3: The B2B Target Audience

Part 3

The B2B Target Audience

Exclusive
ONLINE MASTERCLASS
What's the #1 Mistake on Your Website?

#1: You'll Know the Difference Between Weak and Strong Websites.

#2: The 5 Cs That Make High-Converting Web Content.

#3: Missed Opportunities That Affect How Your Web Content Performs to Attract Traffic and Generate Leads.

Click on the link below (or type the URL into your browser) To Watch a FREE 50-Minute MASTERCLASS.
https://lifesciencecopywriter.com/site-content-audit-masterclass

And get This FREE B2B Content Creation Cheat Sheet.

CHAPTER ELEVEN

The Decision-Making Unit Constitutes Your B2B Target Audience

Quote

"You can't hit a target you
cannot see, and you cannot see
a target you do not have."

~ Zig Ziglar ~
Motivational Speaker, and Author.

People who have similar needs or wants respond similarly to marketing initiatives. So instead of selling to everyone, you need to focus on building a relationship with a specific target audience.

But you cannot define your target audience if you don't know your target market.

The motivational speaker and author ... Zig Ziglar, said ... *"You can't hit a target you cannot see, and you cannot see a target you do not have."*

That's why marketing professionals always start by spending some time defining their target market.

What Is The Right Target Market For Your Offer?

According to Investopedia.com ... *"A target market is a group of customers with shared demographics who are the most likely buyers of a product or service"*.

It comprises people broadly categorized by age, location, income, and lifestyle.

This is a high-level, zoomed-out view of who buys your product.

But one of the best ways to identify your target market is to start with your offer. Then look at competing websites, social media, and marketing materials.

Examine your industry's publications, market reports, and statistics as well.

And so your target market should be ...

1. *Identifiable:*
   That means that you should be able to describe it according to ...
   - Geographic characteristics like the country, region, city, suburbs, or climate,
   - Demographic characteristics like gender, age, employment status, income, family, or social status,
   - Psychographic traits like personality, aptitude, lifestyle, values, or
   - Consumer behavioral considerations like usage, loyalty, buyer readiness, and preferences.

2. *Accessible:*
   Look at the business environment, including regulatory restrictions. If your product faces a lot of red tape, maybe that market is not accessible to your business.

3. *Substantial:*
   It should be large enough to enable you to make a tidy profit.

4. *Measurable:*
   You should know your market share, purchasing power, and position in the industry.

Choosing the right target market means narrowing your audience down to a group of customers within a segment. They should have shared demographics and be the most likely buyers of your product or service.

To illustrate this point, let's look at Table 11.1, which was extracted from the "*2022 Global Life Sciences Outlook*" report. In this report, the Life Science market was divided into five different end-user segments.

Each end-user segment of the life science market has different target markets.

For example ...

Clinical Laboratory Diagnostic is a target market in the Life Science Research and Laboratory segment.

You can focus your marketing message on the people most likely to buy your product ... that is ... your target audience.

But if you choose the wrong target market ... for instance, Pharmaceutical Companies ... you won't identify the right target audience for your Clinical Laboratory Diagnostic products.

Table 11.1: 5 End-User Segments of the Life Science Market.

---

1. Biotech & Pharmaceutical Companies. These include ...

- Biotechnology Companies,
- Pharmaceutical Companies, and
- Biopharmaceutical Companies.

2. Medical Devices/Instruments/Equipment/Products. Including ...

- Diagnostic apparatus,
- Medical Appliances and Instruments,
- Medical Equipment and Machines, and
- Medical Consumables, Reagents, and Products.

3. Scientific Equipment. These include ...

- Capital Instruments and Equipment, and
- Non-capital Machinery & Disposable Supplies.

4. Life Science Research and Laboratory Services. These include ...

- Clinical Laboratory Diagnostic Services,
- Contract Research Organizations (CROs),
- Academic & Research Institutions, and
- Forensic Science Testing Laboratories.

5. Food & Beverage Companies. These include ...

- Dairy Processing,
- Probiotics,
- Brewing Companies, and
- Genetic engineering approaches to enhance food quality.

Unmet Needs Open Up Opportunities To Serve The Right Target Audience

Your products and services will fail in the market if there's a misalignment between the solutions you offer and what your buyer's true needs are.

Because, like many businesses, you may have a narrow definition of who makes up your target audience.

Many businesses make the mistake of defining their target audience by geography, demographics, products, technology, or application.

Many others define their target audience by their existing customers and the products they buy.

As a result, there has always been disagreement about the definition of a target audience. Because through their company's lens, they find it hard to see how best to define their audience.

However, if you use the 'Jobs-To-Be-Done' approach, you will find it easier to come up with a more practical definition of your target audience.

According to Anthony W. Ulwick … founder and chief executive officer of Strategyn ... the definition of your target audience should be "*A group of people plus the job they want to get done*".

And since people buy products or services to get a job done, it would serve you better to define your audience through a 'Jobs-To-Be-Done' lens.

Remember that your prospects are NOT a market. Not 'The pharmaceutical industry' or 'environmental labs'. They are human beings.

So the definition of your target audience should describe the people who make purchasing decisions.

Greater specificity of who they are will permit greater filtering and support clearer messaging in your marketing content, which will result in better outreach.

The 'Jobs-To-Be-Done' framework is a perspective. A powerful lens that will help you observe markets, segment buyers, and view competitors differently.

And in doing so, you can make the success of your marketing content far more predictable.

Thus, the 'Jobs-To-Be-Done' framework forces you to change your mindset and think more broadly. It suggests focusing on the job your buyers hope to do by hiring your product.

In the Clinical Laboratory Diagnostic unit example …
- The Laboratory Director wants to replace his stock,
- The Quality Manager wants to meet certification standards, and
- The Bench Technologist wants an easy-to-use diagnostic kit.

In a Harvard Business Review article, Clayton M. Christensen, Scott Cook, and Taddy Hall reported that ... *"The structure of a market, seen from the buyers' point of view, is simple. They just need to get things done"*.

When these people buy your product, they bring it in to help them do a job. And if it does the job well, they will get it again. But if it doesn't, they will look for something else that can solve their problem.

And so ...

Defining your target audience from the perspective of a problem space ... rather than a solution space ... will offer you a stable, long-term focal point for value creation. Because while products come and go, what people want to do remains constant in the equation.

But most importantly, the 'Jobs-To-Be-Done' argument can help you define your buyers' unmet needs.

And similarly, the definition of what your buyers need may not be clear through your company's lens. However, when viewed through the lens of the 'Jobs-To-Be-Done' framework, it becomes clear.

People don't have latent needs. They can articulate exactly what they are trying to do. They buy products or services to get a job done.

Thus, it is important to define your buyers' needs as the measurable outcomes they want to achieve once they get the job done.

For example ...
- The Laboratory Director wants to ensure that his staff has equipment,
- The Quality Manager wants to achieve compliance status in an audit, and
- The Bench Technologist wants to reduce the turnaround time of a test.

So, what are your buyer's unmet needs?

When you shift your perspective to look at the needs discovery process through the eyes of your buyer, you end up with better results. And the needs statements you develop will guide you to create valuable marketing content every time you get down to doing it in the future.

116

And … according to Anthony W. Ulwick … through a 'Jobs-To-Be-Done' lens, unmet needs are simply defined as … "*the important measurable outcomes that are not well satisfied by today's solutions*".

Returning to the diagnostic kit example …

You might say that the Bench Technologist buys diagnostic kits to 'conduct specific tests in the lab.' But that's not entirely correct.

The actual job done is to 'help patients get answers about their health status.'

If you reframe the 'Jobs-To-Be-Done' like this, you end up with different content marketing opportunities.

And in the diagnostic kit example …

Rather than focusing on making cheaper diagnostic kits, consider making better kits that give accurate results.

So, figuring out what your buyers want but aren't getting will help you come up with ideas for content that will win the market.

Defining Your Target Audience From The Right Target Market

In the 15th Edition of Marketing Management, Philip Kotler and Kevin Lane Keller say it's impossible to serve a broad market effectively. Because casting a wide net doesn't guarantee you any more closed sales.

And so, promoting your product or service without a specific audience in mind is one of the biggest business mistakes you can make.

Why?

Because it will be a waste of resources to reach everyone since not everyone in your target market is your buyer. And spending time promoting content to a dead-end audience won't enhance your customer acquisition.

Instead, part of being successful in your chosen market is knowing who will like your product and who will ultimately buy it.

So focus your marketing initiatives only on the people likely to buy what you sell. In other words, focus on your target audience.

So, who are these people?

A target audience is a subset of your target market that is made up of people who are likely to buy from you.

And in any situation, the best way to achieve that is to first think about the specific needs your product fulfills. The more specific you can be about figuring out what those needs are, the more specific and targeted your audience will be.

Defining who takes center stage as your target audience comes down to just three simple categories:

1. *A Person's Socio-Demographic Characteristics:*

    In this category, you will look at the age, income, education, profession, gender, or geographic location.

    One way to collect this data is to look at your current customer base.

    You can also gather actionable insights by monitoring your social media analytics for engagement. Also, track metrics like follows, comments, shares, and likes.

    And when you have this data, it becomes easier to find other people like them. These are people who aren't in your circle of influence but have the same characteristics as your target audience. And they could also enjoy your product.

2. *A Person's Hobbies, Passions, Or Interests:*

    Data about your users' hobbies, passions, and interests can provide you with actionable information ... and help you engage your buyers in a way that interests them.

    With this, you can connect with your audience in a way that is relatable to them. You can also unearth behaviors that motivate their buying decisions.

And you can create highly personalized, data-driven messages that will make them feel important, seen, and appreciated. That will make them more loyal to your brand.

3. *A Person's Purchase Intentions, Buying Preferences, Or Spending Power:*

It's always a good idea to start your research by looking at your customer base's analytics. You want to identify likely pain points and determine who experiences them.

Also, establish if they control a budget. This will help you create tailored messaging that addresses their needs.

One benefit of defining a target audience is that it makes it easier for you to perform keyword research that will help you create targeted content. That will help you communicate your marketing message more effectively. The more relevant your content is to your readers, the more persuasive it will be.

From the previous example ... Clinical Laboratory Diagnostic Services ...

If you look at the organizational structure, you will find that the people most likely to make up your target audience in this segment are the people in key staffing positions.

Namely ...
- The Business Manager,
- The Pathologist,
- The Medical Scientist,
- The Laboratory Director,
- The Quality Manager, and
- The Bench Technologist.

But be aware of who isn't your target audience, so you don't waste money promoting your offer to people who are not interested.

The 'Decision-Making Unit' (DMU)

In account-based marketing, the 'Decision-Making Unit' is a team of people who make buying decisions for the organization.

Whereas each unit has certain personas in it, the number of individuals in it varies from one business to another ... and from one sale to another.

But in each sale, all individuals on the team would participate in making decisions and also have influence over which provider wins a bid.

But how often do B2B companies use the 'Decision-Making Unit'?

According to a market research report by Demand Gen, entitled ... *"B2B Buyers Survey"* ... 79% of B2B buying involves a 'Decision-Making Unit' with 2 to 6 personas.

And in another study by InboxInsight, entitled ... *"HR Buying Behavior"* ... 70% of companies surveyed involved 5 or more people in each purchasing process.

But what does this mean to you as a content marketer?

It means that each member of the 'Decision-Making Unit' represents a different slice of your target audience.

In contrast to how individuals making business-to-consumer (B2C) purchases arrive at their buying decisions, members of the 'Decision-Making Unit' collectively contribute to B2B purchase decisions.

So if you know the distribution of labor within this unit, you can predict how an organization's buying process will go.

You will know the extent of the involvement of each person in the 'Decision-Making Unit'. And also how to target each role in your marketing message based on how much they contribute to the overall buying process.

What Roles Do Individual 'Decision-Making Unit' Archetypes Play In Organizational Buying?

You don't want to reach the end of the sales process only to find that your point of contact needs approval from other people ... before they can commit to a sale.

So, instead of exposing yourself to this risk, why not eliminate as much of the unknown as possible?

Sometimes the 'Jobs-To-Be-Done' in specific buying decision-making processes are not tied to any specific job title. So, it is unlikely to find the same team of individuals handling all purchases in an organization.

It can be hard to figure out who sits on the unit at your target accounts. But you need to know who they are to ensure that you can target the right people with your marketing campaigns.

The best way to identify these people is to assign buying roles to them. To see them as characters that perform specific 'Jobs-To-Be-Done', rather than looking at them by the staffing positions they hold.

Knowing who these people are will help frame your sales conversations around their individual pain points. And give you the tools to craft powerful campaign messages that speak to the right people who have a say and can influence the buying decision.

So how can you find out who 'The Decision-Maker' is? Using the 'Jobs-To-Be-Done' framework.

This will reveal the following 5 archetypes:

1. *'The Initiator' or The Executive Sponsor:*

    This is the person who will recognize that the unmet need in the organization is a problem. He will be the first to suggest the need to purchase a product to help resolve that issue ... thus triggering the start of the purchase decision-making process. And in our Clinical Laboratory Diagnostic Services market example, this role would be assigned to the Laboratory Director. He is in charge of the inventory and will place an order for a depleted item in the stock. He is the 'enthusiast' in the adoption curve. He feels duty-bound to find products that will improve their workflow.

2. *'The Influencer' or The Supporter:*

    This is the person whose opinion or recommendation influences the decision to buy. Often, 'The Influencer' is a subject matter expert. The most technically astute member of the team. He exerts influence by establishing preconditions. He researches options, highlights product specifications, and provides information that sets the criteria for evaluating alternatives. But he doesn't hold the budget and has no authority to act alone or make a final decision. But he can draw in key stakeholders ... such as finance or IT ... throughout the sales process. He can also sway other people in their decision-making roles. And so you need to provide him with resources so he can argue your case better. In our example, 'The Influencer' can be the Pathologist or Medical Scientist ... depending on the specific need. He is the 'visionary' in the adoption curve. A true product evangelist.

3. *The End-User*:

This is the person who will use and work with the purchased goods. He is likely to be the one who will identify an unmet need and propose a solution to be found. He is concerned about performance and ease of use. He may not have a say in the buying process. Neither does he have decision-making authority. However, one end-user can influence the others to impact the sales process. In our example, this role belongs to the Bench Technologist. He is the 'pragmatist' in the adoption curve. More cautious and needs honest facts.

4. *The Blocker* or *The Veto Power Holder*:

This person has the veto power to stop the sales process from moving forward. He has all the qualities of an influencer. He will also play a key role in researching solutions. He resists the final selection of what to buy, where to buy it, and when to buy it. And he will object to the purchase if he is not convinced. So he can be tricky to handle. Find out if you will cross paths with him as early as possible in the sales process. And learn why he might object to the sale. Knowing that can help you overcome his objections and stop him from halting your sale. In our example, the Quality Manager can easily play this role. He is the 'skeptic' in the adoption curve. Not easily convinced. He needs some extra handholding.

5. *The Decision-Maker* or *The Budget-Holder*:

In any purchase, you have one decision-maker at a time. Also called the decider or the buyer. This is the person who signs the check that pays for the purchase. As the decider, he chooses the supplier. As the buyer, he has the formal responsibility to negotiate and the authority to sign contracts with vendors. He might even conduct his own independent research on the solutions being considered. And he will often delegate the buying process to 'The Influencer' until it moves further along. This is the C-suite that signs the check and allocates resources. So if you can't reach him right away, try talking to 'The Influencer'. Ultimately, 'The Decision-Maker' makes the final decision to purchase. In our example, the Business Manager plays this role. He is the 'conservative' on the adoption curve. And cautious when he has to spend on a tight budget.

While 'The End-User' and 'The Decision-Maker' can be defined and identified relatively easily ... based on their organizational tasks ... the other roles 'The Initiator', 'The Influencer', and 'The Blocker' are much more difficult to identify. You will have to resort to their roles in the buying process to define them.

In larger organizations, you might also encounter 2 peripheral 'Decision-Making Unit' roles.

The first peripheral role is ...

6. *'The Gatekeeper':*
   This person works closely with 'The Decision-Maker'. He handles administrative duties as the executive assistant, administrative assistant, secretary, or receptionist. He controls the flow of information to 'The Decision-Maker' and determines the type of information delivered. So, don't try to get past him. Instead, align with him. Be polite and treat him as a resource rather than an obstacle.

The second peripheral role is ...

7. *'Legal and Compliance':*
   This is the person responsible for the contract terms and conditions. He doesn't act as a blocker but can slow down the sales process when he gets involved in the later stages. This might be the Chief Financial Officer (CFO). He needs to review and approve the contract. Maybe the procurement department needs to ensure compliance. Regardless of what that approval process looks like, he can help you forecast when a sale closes.

These 5 (or sometimes 7) archetypes collectively constitute the 'Decision-Making Unit' with members often drawn from different departments. It is rightly called the buying center, and these people are effectively ... your target audience ... your buyers.

But targeting the 'Decision-Making Unit' does not mean you must exclude every other person who doesn't meet your criteria. On the contrary, targeting allows you to focus your message on the right people most likely to influence a purchase.

Knowing who sits in the 'Decision-Making Unit' will make it easier for you to gather information about them. And so any information you can collect about the persons involved can be helpful.

When you understand the 'Jobs-To-Be-Done', you can plan your content messaging approach. And since each member has unique information requirements, you can tailor your content to deliver the right message at the right time throughout the buying decision-making process

---

The Key Takeaways from Chapter 4:

1. A target market is a group of customers with shared demographics who are the most likely buyers of a product or service

2. A target audience is a subset of people in your target market who represent your potential buyer base.

3. Your buyer's needs are the measurable outcomes they want to achieve once they get the job done.

Coming Up In The Next Chapter ...

Data-driven insights into the Decision-Making Unit archetypes.

CHAPTER TWELVE

Data-Driven Insights Into The Decision-Making Unit Archetypes

Quote

"Content marketing is no
longer a numbers game. It's
a game of relevance."

~ Jason Miller ~
Communications Strategist.

The effectiveness of your marketing depends on how well you can leverage buyer insights to tailor a continuum of content that acts as a companion your buyers can look to ... when they need help to make an informed judgment ... at each step of their buying decision-making process.

Having easy access to this kind of content ... on an ongoing basis ... creates rewarding buying experiences for them.

But it's one thing to claim that you understand your buyers' specific needs... and quite another to make decisions about them when you don't know what they need.

That's why seasoned marketing teams ask before they tell. They gather actionable consumer insights before they present an offer.

Insights Into The Personas Of The 'Decision-Making Unit'

Identifying 'Decision-Making Unit' archetypes is not an end in itself. You still need to understand the organizational decision-making process as a whole.

And since your content targets people in the 'Decision-Making Unit', you should speak to their interests.

You need insights into ...
- The personas that naturally emerge in your market,
- Your target audience's hot buttons,
- The objections that your target audience will naturally raise, and
- The greatest challenges your potential buyers experience.

But how can you generate these insights?

The best discovery method on the market today is the 'Deep-Dive Survey'. This is a counterintuitive process that was created by Ryan Levesque ... author of the #1 best-selling book ... ASK.

The 'Deep-Dive Survey' can be broken down into 2 phases ...

The first phase is quantitative. This is where you identify the division of labor among the archetypes and their relative influence on the buying process. The goal is to categorize the respondents into 5 groups that match the core buying roles of the 'Decision-Making Unit' archetypes.

The second phase is qualitative. This is where you will do a needs and behavioral analysis of the responses. The goal is to uncover each archetype's specific desires, underlying motivations, and triggers. And also to identify discrete sets of information needs.

Once you have those insights, you can then overlay them on the Decision-Making Process.

Be sure to consider the following questions ...
- Will they see a need for your product?
- What drives them to make purchase decisions?
- Can they afford to buy your product?
- Are they easily accessible, so you can reach them with your message?
- At what stage in the buying decision-making process do members participate?
- How does the group circulate information?
- How much authority does each group member have?
- Who has the power to make the final decision? And ...
- How do motivations differ among different members?

Answering these questions will make it easier for you to tailor a continuum of content for each step of the buying process. You want to reach the right people and speak directly to the stage-specific interests of all your buyers in a layered manner.

These insights can help you have more meaningful communication and build stronger relationships. You can project future consumption behavior. And generate data that lays the foundation for all the elements of your content marketing.

They can also serve as a 'cheat sheet' to inspire business action and grow your brand exponentially. And they make all the difference between a healthy bottom line and a floundering business.

Ultimately, this will smooth the buying process, resulting in a shorter sales cycle. Yielding better returns on your marketing investment will help you have higher win rates for your team and put more money in your bank.

So, let's get into the details of how you can apply the 'Deep-Dive Survey' to your target audience.

A 'Deep-Dive Survey' For Actionable Insights Into The 'Decision-Making Unit'

Consumer insights provide an easy way to understand your target audience.

But before you build your 'Deep-Dive Survey', you should establish what you want to achieve. You need to be clear about your goal ... your WHY.

What Ryan Levesque calls your Deep-Dive WHY.

But what do you really want to uncover? What outcome do you expect for your business?

Imagine that you had to choose one of the 4 scenarios below. Which one would apply to your business the most?

1. *Focus On A New Target Audience:*
   - You'd like to discover a NEW TARGET AUDIENCE, or
   - You want to know if the TARGET AUDIENCE you have discovered is worth pursuing.

2. *Focus On An Existing Target Audience:*
   - You want to uncover blind spots in your EXISTING TARGET AUDIENCE, or
   - You want to reveal the challenges your EXISTING TARGET AUDIENCE is facing.

3. *Focus On A New Offer (Product Or Service):*
   - You want to figure out the best NEW OFFER you can develop, or
   - You want to be sure that the NEW OFFER you have in mind is worth developing.

4. *Focus On An Existing Offer (Product Or Service):*
   - You want to unearth what might be missing in your EXISTING OFFER, or
   - You want to uncover why people choose not to buy your EXISTING OFFER.

The great thing about your choice is that it will help you know where your goal falls along the TARGET AUDIENCE-to-OFFER spectrum (as illustrated in Figure 12.1).

Figure 12.1: The target audience-to-offer spectrum

So now that you know that your 'Deep-Dive Survey' focuses on ...

- A new target audience,
- An existing target audience,
- A new offer, or
- An existing offer.

What can you do with this information?

It boils down to two choices ...

- You either want to gain insights that will help you learn more about your TARGET AUDIENCE, or
- You want to know if your OFFER is a good fit for your target audience.

But it always works better to think of your goal as falling along a spectrum ... with a TARGET AUDIENCE FOCUS on one end and an OFFER FOCUS on the other.

Where your goal falls on this spectrum depends on ...

- Whether you're looking for information about your TARGET AUDIENCE or your OFFER, or
- Whether your TARGET AUDIENCE or OFFER IS NEW OR EXISTING.

Here's How The 'Deep-Dive Survey' Works ...

The 'Deep-Dive Survey' is a vital step in your content marketing process. It's all about discovering what makes your ideal buyer tick.

So if you have an existing list of email subscribers, you can set up the survey by writing an email to invite your subscribers to take it. Analyze the responses to determine to which category they belong.

The goal is to get to the point where 80% of the responses fall into 5 different buckets that align with the 5 archetypes of the 'Decision-Making Unit'.

This will come in handy later, when you start customizing your marketing messaging.

But let's say you don't have an existing list of email subscribers, you can use paid Adverts to drive cold traffic to a landing page on your website. You can target people who fit the description of your audience to take your 'Deep-Dive Survey'.

Whichever way you do it, the beauty of the 'Deep-Dive Survey' is the accuracy with which it paints a picture of what your target audience is really struggling with. It does not give you room to assume that you know more about your buyer than you really do.

Which is good because you can learn more about what your buyer really needs from your offer and make data-driven decisions that benefit your content marketing strategy.

But the outcome of your 'Deep-Dive Survey' will depend on the questions asked.

So beware of asking the wrong questions that yield misleading data.

Take this for example ...

Henry Ford, the founding father of Ford Motor Company, once said, "*If I had asked people what they wanted, they would have told me ... faster horses*".

What does this tell you?

Most people who run surveys make the fundamental mistake of not paying attention to the nuances of language when framing their survey questions.

Such mistakes can make or break the survey because subtle linguistic differences will generate different outcomes.

From our experience, we have learned that the best questions to ask are always open-ended. It takes a particular and counterintuitive approach to get it right.

It's all about psychographics and buyers experiences.

And with the right questions asked, you should see the responses naturally coalesce into themes. You get better answers, which reveal what your buyers really need from your business.

The beauty of the 'Deep-Dive Survey' is that it will give you an accurate picture of what your target audience is struggling with. The foremost benefit is that you won't assume to know more about your buyer than you do.

So, when is it most effective to run your 'Deep-Dive Survey'?

It works best before you enter any new market, before you create or launch a brand new product, or before you begin a new content marketing campaign.

Maybe you would like to know if a new business idea is something worth pursuing ... if a new product is worth developing. Or you want to research more about a new market or find out if something is missing from your existing market.

In this initial phase, the key to your marketing success depends on how your survey turns out.

Uncovering The Subconscious Thinking Of The 'Decision-Making Unit' Archetypes To Reveal Actionable Consumer Insights

Customer feedback is the gold mine that makes the 'Deep-Dive Survey' format especially useful.

A needs and behavioral analysis of the feedback will give you insights into how the decision archetypes view themselves. It will also help you uncover their specific needs, desires, underlying motivations, and triggers.

So the most significant feedback to look out for is that of the hyper-respondents.

As a rule of thumb ... if someone pours their heart out, pay attention to them. These are the people who submit the most passionate, detailed, and open-ended responses. They're going to give you some fascinating consumer insights.

The reason is that hyper-respondents are the people in your market who are most likely to buy ... even though they complain the most.

They complain because they still want to buy your product, but they don't like something about it.

How can you get into the mind of your business buyer to figure out what makes him tick?

Once you analyze this data, you'll understand how each respondent self-identifies. This allows you to segment your buyers into 5 buckets based on their alignment with decision-making duties.

And later, you'll be able to come up with data-driven ways to target individuals in each of the 5 buckets with relevant marketing content.

This is where your survey responses come to life. Your audience is telling you exactly what stops them from buying your product, and they want you to listen to them.

You want to focus on the depth of those responses ... to find nuggets and insights that could guide your marketing initiatives.

For example, they will get you to ...

- See the world through the eyes of your buyer.
- Determine if there's demand within the market for your offer.
- Discover what people want to buy.
- Determine the language that you should use to promote your offer.
- Identify the segment in your market.
- And much, much, more!

What a gift this is!

Now, you can have a deeper understanding of what interests each of the 'Decision-Making Unit' archetypes. You can leverage these insights to anticipate their buying behaviors and create targeted content.

And so, it's not enough to simply describe your product and its features or benefits. You must tailor your copy to speak intelligently to the conversations your buyers already have in their heads.

Conversations like …
- How they arrive at buying decisions for their company.
- The information they need to know about your product or service.
- The factors that influence their decision to buy or recommend your product.
- What motivates them to say YES or NO to your offer.

This stuff works! How much more persuasive can it get than that?

I'm sure you've ever encountered timely promotional content that spoke directly to your specific need at the time.

How did that make you feel?

If you have little or no experience with your target audience, think about what you're acquiring.

You're not just learning about email addresses; you're gaining so much access to actionable data about your potential business buyers.

A 'Deep-Dive Survey' can help you decrease your marketing costs and increase your return on investment … though it's going to take a while to do all the work.

But your target audience is not an end in itself. You now have to zoom into your target audience to discover their actionable buyer personas.

The Key Takeaways from Chapter 5:

1. The 'Decision-Making Unit' is the team of individuals in your target audience who play key roles in the B2B buying process.

2. The success of your marketing efforts depends on your ability to understand the specific needs of your buyers. And the language you use in those efforts should resonate with their interests.

3. A 'Deep-Dive Survey' is a counterintuitive discovery process. It will give you accurate insights into your buyer's unmet needs.

4. When is it suitable to run your 'Deep-Dive Survey'? Before you enter any new market, before you create or launch a new product, or before you start a new content marketing campaign.

Coming Up In The Next Chapter ...

Actionable Buyer Personas Of Decision-Making Unit Archetypes.

CHAPTER THIRTEEN

Actionable Buyer Personas Of Decision-Making Unit Archetypes

$$\mathcal{Q}uote$$

"When you combine the Buyer
Profile with Buying Insights,
you will have clear guidance
for the decisions you need to
make to win their business."

~ Adele Revella ~
Keynote speaker and CEO of Buyer
Persona Institute.

According to Aberdeen Strategy & Research, businesses that use personas have 20% conversions compared to 12% conversions among those that don't use personas. That's 73% higher conversions for using personas.

But how can you create such personas?

In the last chapter, we identified five 'Decision-Making Unit' archetypes in the Clinical Laboratory Diagnostic Services market. Just to remind you …

1. 'The Initiator' (assigned to the laboratory director).
2. 'The Influencer' (could be the pathologist or medical scientist).
3. 'The Blocker' (assigned to the quality manager).
4. 'The Decision'-Maker (assigned to the business manager), and
5. 'The End-User' (assigned to the bench technologist).

In that sector, these are the individuals that make up the target audience. So they are the pool of people who would form the buyer base when you target the Clinical Laboratory Diagnostic Services market.

To construct actionable buyer personas for each archetype in this example, you will need insights into how each individual in the 'Decision-Making Unit' arrives at buying decisions.

These would be insights into their subconscious thinking and purchasing behavior.

It would be nice to have actual words from real people looking to your company for solutions. Because those words would reflect the unique attitudes of your target buyers.

To avoid guessing … or creating personas based on your opinions, assumptions, or perceptions … you can choose from any of the three ways below to gather accurate insights into your buyers so you can develop actionable personas for your 'Decision-Making Unit' archetypes …

1. *Market research.*
   This will give you insights into purchase behavior, demographics, consumer preferences, economic trends, industry trends, and market conditions.

2. *Customer feedback.*
   You can get this from comments, surveys, or reviews will give you insights into your buyer experiences.

3. *Tracking website and social media analytics*
   This will give you data-driven insights into user behavior and popular content.

This data will help you identify content opportunities. And empower you to tailor your strategy to target the audience more effectively.

It can help you identify areas to enhance the user experience for increased conversions and retention. And allow you to leverage positive feedback as testimonials and social proof. To build trust and credibility with prospects.

And even though you can make a few educated assumptions, you must be as specific as possible. You want to provide details about their aspirations, needs, objections, and pain points. To identify specific triggers that motivate them to buy.

Because the more detail you provide, the better you and your perfect buyer … the 'Decision-Making Unit' … can connect.

Business-To-Business (B2B) Marketers Can Use More Than One Buyer Persona

Best practice in B2B marketing demands that organizations create separate buyer personas for each archetype. And that the number of buyer personas they develop should equal the number of 'Decision-Making Unit' archetypes.

Because each archetype plays a different purchasing role.

But they must not be identified by job titles alone, because even though organizations might use similar-sounding job titles, actual people with buying roles may differ from titleholders from one organization to another.

What you need to do is develop separate buyer personas for each role. This will help you create targeted content that supports specific responsibilities of the decision-making process rather than staffing positions.

Take the example of a company that sells software to design engineers. Their customers ... who are installers ... have a strong voice in vendor choice. However, the purchase orders often go to executives who ask for additional justification from design engineers.

In this example, the company needs three personas to drive the company to buy their software. So, if they have only one persona ... let's say ... the design engineers ... it would mean the company considers that it has only one customer segment. They will miss out on the opportunity to create content for both the installers and executives.

The use of more than one buyer persona is supported by market research from the Demand Gen B2B Buyers Survey, which showed that 79% of B2B buying involves a 'Decision-Making Unit' with 2 to 6 personas.

A Planner For Creating Buyer Personas For The Decision-Making Unit Roles

How can you use 'Decision-Making Unit' insights to create actionable buyer personas?

Enter all the personas into a spreadsheet in side-by-side columns.

Then build a matrix that answers the questions in tables 13.1 to 13.4 below for each archetype:

Table 13.1: Demographic Characteristics (*Who are they?*)

Action Point	Question
1. Archetype's Name	*Question*: What is the archetype's name? *Reason Why*: A descriptive, alliterative name is memorable.
2. Gender	*Question*: Male? Female? Etc. *Reason Why*: Gender influences their purchase behavior.
3. Age Range	*Question*: In what age range do they belong? *Reason Why*: This will help you create targeted content.
4. Relationship Status	*Question*: Single? Married? Partnered? Separated? Divorced? *Reason Why*: Helps you find new angles to create relevant messages.
5. No. of Children	*Question*: How many children do they have? *Reason Why*: Helps you find new angles to create relevant messages.
6. Education Level.	*Question*: What education level have they achieved? *Reason Why*: Helps you find new angles to create relevant messages.

Table 13.2: Geographic Characteristics (*Where are they?*)

Action Point	Question
7. Location? Region, country, state, ZIP code.	*Question*: Where are they located? *Reason Why*: This can help you tailor your content for relevance.

Table 13.3: Behavioral Characteristics (*What do they do?*)

Action Point	Question
8. Job Title / Position	*Question*: What job title or position do they hold? *Reason Why*: Helps you better understand their needs.
9. Job Responsibilities	*Question*: What duties and responsibilities are attached to their role? *Reason Why*: This helps to reveal their job roles and responsibilities.
10. Annual Income	*Question*: How much do they earn for the role? *Reason Why*: Helps you find new angles to create relevant messages.
11. Hobbies and Interests	*Question*: What are their interests? *Reason Why*: Knowing what interests them will help you build empathy.
12. Media Platform Preferences	*Question*: What social media platforms do they prefer to use? *Reason Why*: This will inform your content distribution strategy.

Table 13.4: Psychographic Characteristics (*What are they?*)

Action Point	Question
13. Your Buyer's Core Problem (Their Unmet Needs)	*Question*: What measurable outcomes do they desire to achieve once they get the job done? *Reason Why*: You want to show them what success looks like.
14. Pain Points	*Question*: What paint points do they experience from their unmet needs? *Reason Why*: Unmet needs can trigger them to start looking for solutions.
15. 'Jobs-To-Be-Done'	*Question*: What are they trying to accomplish? *Reason Why*: People buy products to get a job done. For example … they don't want to buy a quarter-inch drill, they want a quarter-inch hole.
16. Biggest Benefit	*Question*: What's the biggest benefit they get when your product solves their problem? *Reason Why*: Highlighting benefits helps increase conversions.

17. *Product Awareness Level*	*Question*: Are they most aware, product aware, solution aware, problem aware, or completely unaware? *Reason Why*: This informs how to lead your communication strategy.
18. *Primary Decision Stage*	*Question*: At what stage are they involved in the buying process? *Reason Why*: Use this to factor their concerns into the content you share.
19. *Secondary Decision Stage*	*Question*: At what stage are they involved in the buying process? *Reason Why*: Use this to factor their concerns into the content you share.
20. *Influence On Buying Decision*	*Question*: On a scale of 1 to 10, what's their influence on the buying decision? *Reason Why*: Helps you prioritize where to focus the resources allocated to content creation.
21. *Decision Questions Asked*	*Question*: What questions do they ask during the buying process? *Reason Why*: This relates to their role in the 'Decision-Making Unit'.
22. *Budget Controlled*	*Question*: How much budget do they control? *Reason Why*: A budget-holder will have more say in the final decision.
23. *Common Sales Objections*	*Question*: What are their objections? What would stop them from buying? (Pricing? Budget?) *Reason Why*: Unchallenged objections can stop the purchase.
24. *Personal Goals That Influence Their Buying Decision*	*Question*: How will the product help them achieve their personal goals? *Reason Why*: This allows you to identify opportunities to deliver personalized value and build trust.
25. *Organizational Factors That Influence Their Buying Decision*	*Question*: What organizational factors influence their buying decision? *Reason Why*: These factors may constrain them as they make buying decisions.
26. *Decision Criteria*	*Question*: What finally pushes them to make a purchase decision? *Reason Why*: You want to know the emotion that drives their purchase decision.

| 27. *Information Needs* | *Question*: What type of information helps them make a buying decision?
Reason Why: Each 'Decision-Making Unit' persona has unique information needs. |
| 28. *Social Kudos* | *Question*: Who does your buyer want to impress? Line managers? Peers? Senior board members?
Reason Why: Social praise is a major incentive for most employees. |

What you end up with is a one-page 'Decision-Making Unit' buyer persona datasheet, with action points and questions in the first column and archetype-specific entries from the second to fifth columns (as illustrated in Table 13.5).

You can use this matrix as a cross-reference that informs your marketing content.

Table 13.5: Buyer personas matrix example.

Buyer Personas Planner – B2B Decision-Making Unit (DMU)					
	The Initiator	The Influencer	The End-User	The Blocker	The Decision-Maker
Action Point #1 QUESTION: REASON WHY:					
Action Point #2 QUESTION: REASON WHY:					
Action Point #3 QUESTION: REASON WHY:					

How 'Decision-Making Unit' Personas Inform Your Marketing Content

There are many instances where people in the 'Decision-Making Unit' refuse to engage with salespeople directly. In such situations, content marketing is the best way to reach them.

You can position your content with problem-solving messages to encourage engagement. And then track your analytics for proof that different buyers are accessing content on your website.

This removes friction during the sales cycle and makes your marketing job easier.

The personas provide realistic composites that represent your typical buyers. And because you want to nurture them through your sales funnel, you need to understand their purchasing roles.

Rather than targeting the budget holder alone, speak also to other members of the 'Decision-Making Unit'. Because the different archetypes influence the same purchase decision ... especially when the procurement involves a big-ticket item.

But in B2B marketing, you can easily lose sight of people in staff positions and market to the business itself.

In the State of Content Marketing 2022 Global Report, SEMRUSH gives us a way to handle this.

One of the key takeaways from this report was that relevant content should be founded on two things ...
1. Customer research.
2. Empathy for your buyers.

Notice that the emphasis here is on the people ... not the business.

We've already seen how you can build your buyer personas with the help of in-depth customer research.

But what does empathy for your buyers entail?

The goal of using personas is to gain insight into how your buyers think and predict how they will act, respond, and behave.

Their values, attitudes, and interests will pinpoint the exact emotions that push them to buy. And the psychographic traits will help you define their subconscious thoughts.

Empathy means that you can connect with your B2B buyers on a human and personal level. So if you want your content marketing to be successful, start by treating your buyer personas as real human beings ... and then personalize your messages.

That's the whole purpose of this exercise.

You also want to clarify who you don't want to serve ... the people in your target audience who are not a good fit for your business.

Knowing who these people are can help you create marketing content that speaks to the right people in a layered manner. Each 'Decision-Making Unit' persona enters the buying process at different stages. Each requires supportive information for their role.

But without buyer personas, you will essentially be guessing what your ideal buyers need. Guessing reduces the effectiveness of your content marketing campaigns.

Knowing your buyers at the human level makes all the difference between having a connection and communicating in a void.

People love to focus their attention on themselves and their situations. And so your content should mirror the conversations that start in their heads ... not yours.

Your content needs to hit all the right buttons and still be interesting and relevant to them.

How?

Having buyer personas allows you to write customized content. You can tailor it to match the roles and interests of each 'Decision-Making Unit' archetype.

As a marketer, you need to look at your buyer's experience as a whole. So that whenever you create content, you can anticipate their needs. And provide answers to their question ... *What's in it for me?*

And that's exactly what each buyer wants ... to feel seen, heard, and acknowledged. It's your job to make that happen.

Your content should be customer-centric, genuinely helpful, and even comforting. To put the spotlight on them in your marketing.

It should also cover all stages of the buying decision-making process.

What do you gain from creating personalized content for your buyers?

In a study by Small Business Trends, 55% of marketers said that personalization made their conversion rates go up. And in a HubSpot study, personalized content delivered 18 times more profit than standard content.

In 1960, Jerome McCarthy formulated the 7 Ps of marketing. These tactics are still applicable today, and you can use them to personalize your content.

They are ...

- Product: The product or service your business is selling.
- Price: The pricing strategy, discounts, terms, fees, etc.
- Promotion: Content marketing, ads, and sales tactics for awareness.
- Place: Where you make, sell, or distribute your products.
- People: Your customers and your sales and marketing staff.
- Process: How you deliver your product or service to your customer.
- Physical evidence: What your customers see when interacting with your business. Including your packaging, branding, physical environment, and interior design.

If you can personalize these elements, you will offer products or services that meet your buyer's specific needs or wants ... and increase your sales and profits too.

Such content will be the single most important asset your business can have.

The Key Takeaways from Chapter 6:

1. B2B buying involves a 'Decision-Making Unit' with 2 to 6 personas. And each 'Decision-Making Unit' archetype plays a different purchase decision-making role.

2. The buyer personas of 'Decision-Making Unit' members can glean insights into purchasing behavior.

3. The goal of using personas is to gain insight into how your buyers think. To predict how they act, respond, and behave. So you can write customized content that is tailored to match the roles and interests of the 'Decision-Making Unit' archetypes.

Coming Up In The Next Chapter ...

PART 4: A Continuum of Empathy-Based Educational Content.

Part 4

A Continuum of Empathy-Based Educational Content

Exclusive

ONLINE MASTERCLASS

What's the #1 Mistake on Your Website?

#1: You'll Know the Difference Between Weak and Strong Websites.

#2: The 5 Cs That Make High-Converting Web Content.

#3: Missed Opportunities That Affect How Your Web Content Performs to Attract Traffic and Generate Leads.

Click on the link below (or type the URL into your browser) To Watch a FREE 50-Minute MASTERCLASS.
https://lifesciencecopywriter.com/site-content-audit-masterclass

And get This FREE B2B Content Creation Cheat Sheet.

CHAPTER FOURTEEN

Beyond The Traditional Marketing Funnel

$$\mathcal{Q}uote$$

"You cannot bore people
into buying your product;
you can only interest them
in buying it."

~ David Mackenzie Ogilvy CBE ~
Founder of Ogilvy & Mather &
The "Father of Advertising."

Most marketers learn that both the sales funnel and the buyer's journey take on a linear shape. They start at the top with awareness, then move down to the consideration stage, and finally end at the decision to buy.

However, linear models are no longer realistic in the digital marketplace.

In 2018, Google published a report entitled *"Beyond the traditional marketing funnel: a new formula for growth"*.

They looked at thousands of user clickstream data over 6 months and found 3 surprising outcomes …

1. The paths that most buyers took were not linear and didn't resemble the cone shape of the classic sales funnel,
2. Instead, the journeys most buyers took looked more like pyramids, diamonds, hourglasses, or even other shapes, and
3. No two buyers had similar paths in their customer journeys.

While the traditional marketing funnel expects people to go through multiple phases of the funnel in a predetermined sequential order, the Google finding explains how intent-rich moments are altering the shape of the marketing funnel.

And now, with 24/7 mobile usage, people have access to a wealth of information online, giving them the power to research and evaluate their options thoroughly before making purchase decisions.

They expect immediate answers in the moments they want to learn, discover, or buy. And every time they turn to digital devices for assistance, they signal their intent.

The challenge for you is to know your customers well enough to predict their search intent. You need to anticipate what your target audience will search for at each stage of the buying decision-making process.

By understanding their information-seeking behavior, you can tailor your content to address the needs of your target audience at each stage. This will enable you to create content that is both helpful and relevant.

And help you build strong relationships that will drive your business activities by …

1. Attracting traffic,
2. Generating leads, and
3. Converting leads into paying customers.

Content That Matches Search Intent At Each Stage Of The Buying Process Ranks High in Google Search Results

While the goal of every content marketing strategy has always been to drive growth through conversions, with the marketing funnel no longer linear, the formula for achieving that has changed.

What will it take for your content to be visible in Google search results?

The answer is simple …

Optimization!

What does that mean?

The #1 goal of the Google algorithm is to return the most relevant results that match the search intent. However, it often updates its algorithm to ensure that it can continue to match what users search for with relevant content.

And because of how content shows up in the search results, Google cares more about prioritizing content that matches a user's search intent. It gives them the most unique and relevant content that matches their search.

For Google, it's all about helping web users find what they look for online at any particular moment. It does not prioritize how you optimize your content.

The only way your prospect will find your content is if it ranks highly, especially on the first page of their Google search results listing.

When optimizing your content, you need to know how people use Google search. And how they type in queries when they want to research, compare, or buy.

So, your top priority should be to keep your buyer's search intent in mind.

There are important things you must do when optimizing your content to ensure that it meets both your buyers' search intent and Google's algorithm requirements.

When selecting the most relevant content, the Google algorithm prioritizes 5 elements ...

1. The page title,
2. A meta description that summarizes what your webpage contains,
3. The headline,
4. Descriptive body text that conveys valuable information to a user, and
5. Keywords that match what users search for.

So, if your content contains all the elements, it will be highly ranked, and the user may click the link to your site.

As a marketer, that's what you want.

But you can no longer base your content approach on a linear buyer's journey because whenever web users indicate their search intent, they redefine and reshape your marketing funnel.

Instead, you must anticipate your prospect's search intent at each stage of the buying decision-making process and optimize your content to serve both intent-rich moments and the Google algorithm.

But beware of creating content that manipulates the Google algorithm. Because Google will delist you from their rankings if they find that you are manipulating their algorithm.

Instead, you should focus on creating content that genuinely benefits the user.

Creating A Content Strategy That Matches Your Buyer's Google Search Intent

Consider this ...

When someone visits Google, they have a specific goal in mind.

Think about all the times you've searched for something online...

You always expect to get back correct answers that match whatever query you put out there. The same is true for your prospective buyers.

As a marketer, you may take this for granted, but having the ability to anticipate search intent makes all the difference in content marketing.

But what exactly is 'search intent'?

This is the primary reason why a web user searches for his problem on Google. It is the motivation behind their quest on Google or any other search engine.

Every time the user types something into a Google search, he has some intent.

Is he looking for specific information? Does he hope to make a purchase? Or is he just browsing the web to find a good deal?

Understanding what a web user wants to find is the key to figuring out the kinds of content they need most.

Google considers a search to be successful when it pulls out the correct information that matches the web user's intent.

Thus, search intent is truly the backbone of a well-optimized content marketing strategy.

Why?

Web users use specific words ... keywords, and key phrases ... to request that search engines supply them with precise information.

And search engines like Google make it their top priority to serve web users by delivering the most relevant and unique content. Content that gives the user answers closest to the question they asked.

But before your prospect gets to read or access your content, they will first see a list of all search results that match their query. You want your content to be on that list ... and as much as possible ... to rank highly.

The higher your content ranks on that list, the greater the chances of the web user clicking on it if it matches his search intent.

To create content that feeds the search intent, you must know where in the buying decision-making process your buyer is. You then align each piece of content with a specific search intent.

As a business, you should care about five main types of search intent.

1. The 'Informational Search Intent' or 'Research Search Intent'.
2. The 'Navigational Search Intent'.
3. The 'Comparison Search Intent'.
4. The 'Transactional Search Intent' or 'Commercial Search Intent'.
5. The 'Succeed Search Intent'.

Let's break down each search intent, and look at examples of how you can use keywords or key phrases to create content that matches a web user's search intent.

1. *The Informational or Research Intent:*

Google is primarily an informational search engine. Informational queries are the most common queries submitted.

People searching with the 'Informational Intent' will generally be in the 'awareness' phase of the sales funnel. At the top of the funnel (TOFU). They want to learn about a broad concept or topic.

When they approach Google, they are looking for educational resources ... which can be simple things like knowing the time or complex things like a strategy guide.

So the 'Informational Intent' involves early-stage search queries. This is where your prospect is researching and trying to learn more about a topic.

In any case, your goal is to educate users about your product or service.

Why?

A website usability study by Small Business Trends showed that 94% of users return to a website if they learn something valuable from it. To them, the site establishes itself as an authoritative source on the topic.

And that user has a higher chance of converting later … when they will be ready.

For Google to understand that your content is informational, it should include keywords or phrases like …

- Examples
- Guide
- How
- Tips
- Tutorial

- What
- When
- Where
- Why

Here are some headlines from actual Thermo Fisher Scientific blogs (https://www.thermofisher.com/blog/) that match the 'Informational Search Intent' queries …

- *"What Do Cells Share in Therapy?"*
- *"How to Get More Out of Your Saliva Collection & Handling."*
- *"14 Tips for a Successful RNA Extraction."*

Providing educational content is a great way to showcase your expertise and build trust with your audience.

2. *The Navigational Intent:*

Part of discovery in the buyer's journey is a search with 'Navigational Intent'. It comes from someone who is aware of your brand.

The goal of their search query will be specific … to locate your website and social media pages so they can find out more about your brand.

Google understands what the user wants and will show your website and physical location without offering ads or special deals.

So if a user is searching for your company, you want them to find you … not your competitors.

You also don't want your keywords to direct people to the navigational searches that promote your competitors. Because … what would be the point of that?

But you must keep track of the ranking to confirm that you show up for your company or brand name … a strong indicator of your brand authority. And this is what your marketing should target.

And so you want to use the following navigational keywords …
- Brand name
- Product name
- Company name
- Service name

Here are some headlines from actual AstraZeneca press releases (https://www.astrazeneca.com/media-centre/press-releases.html) that match the 'Navigational Intent' queries …

- *"AstraZeneca aims to redefine breast cancer care with new data across the treatment spectrum at SABCS 2022."*
- *"AstraZeneca ranked in the top three in the Access to Medicine Index."*

Navigational keywords are all about increasing brand awareness. And ensuring your current customers and future buyers can find you when they need you most.

And so, building a solid brand is the best way to optimize your website for this type of search intent.

You want to become a resource that web users can bookmark and continually visit … not just locate once through a Google search.

3. *The Comparison Intent:*

The 'Comparison Intent' is a hybrid of the 'Informational Intent' and 'Transactional Intent'. It aims to showcase product information, roll out reviews, and compare different products.

People who conduct comparison searches are likely to convert but aren't quite ready to buy. They are looking for products or services from different providers.

They want information that helps them compare your product or service with other offers. But they haven't decided if they will buy or what to buy.

They are simply exploring their options as they decide what to do.

And since they are still defining product requirements, they want to compare all available solutions. Their focus is to consider certain brands so they can select a vendor.

Content that satisfies the 'Comparison Intent' is middle-stage content. And the user is in the consideration stage in the middle of the funnel (MOFU).

Often, 'Comparison Intent' searches include keywords and phrases like ...

- Best
- Compare
- Review
- Specific location
- Top

These are the keywords your audience uses when they're doing research. They need content that will help them define product requirements and compare available solutions ... before making a purchase decision.

But, of course, product comparisons aren't the only type of comparison search. Your buyer also needs evidence to support vendor promises and eliminate solutions that aren't a good fit.

So he will look at reviews, technical specifications, recommendations, free trials, or demonstrations.

Here are examples of headlines from actual Pfizer Inc. blogs (https://www.pfizer.com/news/articles) that match the 'Comparison Intent' queries …

- *"What Makes an RNA Vaccine Different From a Conventional Vaccine?"*
- *"Biologics vs. Biosimilars: Key Differences Explained."*
- *"Understanding the Differences and Similarities Between the Flu and COVID-19."*
- *"The Do's and Don'ts of Wearing a Face Mask."*

How can you optimize content for 'Comparison Intent'?

Compile reviews that compare different products.

Searches with 'Comparison Intent' can also be location-specific. For example … when a user searches for the best sports shop in their next vacation destination.

4. *The Transactional or Commercial Intent:*

At the decision stage … the bottom of the funnel (BOFU) … your prospective buyers will be searching with the 'Transactional Intent'.

Despite what the name implies, searches with the 'Transactional Intent' do not involve purchases alone. They can also lead users to other conversion actions, such as a lead magnet download, a sign-up for a free trial, or a registration for a free webinar.

A 'Transactional Intent' is most likely to result in a conversion or a purchase. So your late-stage content should help your prospects overcome common sales objections. It should also help them justify their decision to convert.

So give them prices, discounts, deals, or even make articles on price comparisons.

Thus, transactional content should include keywords and phrases your prospects use when they're ready to convert. You can include words such as …

- Buy
- Cost
- Order
- Discount
- Coupon
- Deals
- Sale
- Save

- Purchase
- Price
- Download
- Buy + [product name]
- [Product name] + price
- [Product name]
- Discount + [product name]

Here are 2 examples of transactional headlines from random 2022 Black Friday deals ...

- *"Save over $60 on the exceptional SuperTank Pro Power Bank."*
- *"Up to 50% Off Black Friday Deal - Phoneplace Black Friday Month."*

For some searches with 'Transactional Intent', Google returns a carousel of products at the top of the results listing. This allows the user to find more products and information before they buy.

5. *The Succeed Intent:*

The 'Succeed Intent' is like the 'Informational Intent,' except that it serves customers in the post-purchase phase.

Here's where the buyer has already purchased your product, and they're trying to use it right. They need informational content that is specific to their customer support queries.

They may not understand how to use it, so they go back into Google and search for "*How do I use this?*" because no one reads the directions anymore.

This is huge for software companies. For example ...

When a buyer purchases a software license and they don't know how to use it, a lot of times, they will go to Google and ask ...

"How do I do this or that with the software?"

Software companies need to anticipate the 'Succeed Intent' and build content that satisfies it. That should get them to rank highly in the search results.

Why Is 'Search Intent' Important For Your SEO Strategy?

Think about a web user's lifecycle on Google search. For example …

What will a scientist who wants to study signal transduction pathways look for?

First, he needs to know what equipment he needs to set up his experiment. So he searches for *"signal transduction imaging systems"*. This will pull up research intent content in the results.

The next query he might type in is *"fluorescence microscope"*. You can see that the intent is evolving here. The type of content that pops up in the search results changes a little bit. More informational-type research content, but also product options.

When his intent changes and this time he searches for *"fluorescence microscope reviews"*, he gets content that compares fluorescence microscopes from different manufacturers.

And as the intent changes again, he types in *"Leica Vs Zeiss fluorescence microscopes"*. Essentially, he wants to compare fluorescence microscopes from two brands. Now he is getting closer to pulling out his credit card.

To show up in the search results, you need to have content that compares your product to that of competitors. And among the results, Google presents different products with prices.

As he gets sucked deep into the purchasing funnel, at some point he will be ready to buy. He types in *"buy Zeiss Fluorescence Microscope"*. The brand itself should top the list. However, Google gives the user a listing of similar products and their prices.
Finally, let's say he bought the Zeiss Fluorescence Microscope. He uses it for a while, and then the UV lamp breaks. He then turns to Google to search for *"Zeiss Fluorescence Microscope UV lamp replacement"*.

What's happening here is that the results listed keep changing as the search intent changes.

And when he searches for his problem, he wants to find information that is relevant to his search query. So, optimizing your content to match his search intent will help drive him to your content page.

However, how well your content matches the search intent of multiple users will impact your overall ability to rank highly in Google searches.

Because search intent greatly influences how SEO delivers relevant search results to users. Thus, intent optimization will enable your content to eventually attract qualified organic traffic to your site.

As a business looking to improve conversion rates, you should have a variety of content that appeals to each search intent ... across the buying decision-making process.

Why?

A thorough understanding of search intent can help you align your keywords with the user's needs, and help you create content that answers their questions. You also create content that search engines consider valuable and relevant to their rankings.

And the more visible you are to users online, the more likely it is that you will have more of them convert.

So, when you create content, you must first figure out what each search query is trying to do. Use this information to select keywords that align with what your users search for on Google.

And if you keep this in mind, you will offer content that offers a lot of value to your readers.

Now that you know the different types of search intent, you should use the right keywords and write content that matches what people are looking for. You also want to create content that will rank highly in the results.
That way, you can deliver value that matches your buyer's specific interests and also engage visitors better.

And when your readers think your content is useful, it's easier to get them to do what you want them to do. Click on the link to your website, where they can read more of your work.

And that's the whole purpose of content marketing!

The Key Takeaways from Chapter 8:

1. When optimizing your content, your top priority should be to keep your buyer's search intent in mind.

2. To create content that feeds the search intent, you must know where in the buying decision-making process your buyer is. You then align each piece of content with a specific search intent.

3. How well your content matches the search intent of multiple users will impact your ability to rank highly in Google search results.

Coming Up In The Next Chapter ...

The Buying Decision-Making Process In An Organization

CHAPTER FIFTEEN

The Buying Decision-Making Process In An Organization

*Q*uote

"People don't buy for
logical reasons. They buy
for emotional reasons."

~ Zig Ziglar ~
Motivational Speaker, and Author.

Organizational buying is the process businesses go through to buy resources for their operations. It starts with researching and moves on to evaluating, negotiating, obtaining approvals, and closing deals.

And because the process is protracted, it involves multiple stakeholders who make decisions for the company. These are employees from different departments, such as procurement, finance, operations, and users.

As a business-to-business (B2B) content marketer, you want to match your sales funnel stages to their decision-making process. This ensures that you can deliver results based on your business goals.

The Classic Sales Funnel

The classic sales funnel is a marketing concept with three phases ...
- Top-of-the-funnel (TOFU),
- Middle-of-the-funnel (MOFU), and
- Bottom-of-the-funnel (BOFU).

This model assumes that you can attract as many people as possible from your target audience to the top of the funnel. Through advertising, social media, word of mouth, or other traffic sources.

You then push them down to the bottom of the funnel ... and a decent number of them will interact with your brand and become paying customers.

The top of the funnel represents the awareness phase. This is where your potential buyers become aware of your solution for the first time. It is the section of the classic sales funnel that carries the most people ... so it is usually the widest part.

In this phase, your potential buyers are furthest from a purchase decision. So your interaction with them is more informational.

Their focus shifts as they move beyond the awareness phase into the middle of the funnel, where they seek to evaluate products ... and conduct competitive market research.

But since you'll never be able to hold on to everyone who enters the funnel at the top, the sales funnel tapers into a cone shape. This narrowing correlates to inevitable attrition from your sales funnel.

The bottom of the funnel is the decision phase. It is the narrowest part of the funnel and holds the fewest number of people in your sales funnel. The few people who make it to this point are the ones who are closest to making a purchase decision. And they have the highest probability of becoming paying customers.

So your interaction with them at this point should be more transactional.

Though the funnel shape suggests that the relationship with your buyers ends at sales, that isn't right. In reality, the sales funnel phases extend beyond purchasing into a post-purchase phase.

Unlike the classic sales funnel, which works on the assumption that there are only 3 stages … top, medium, and bottom … the modern sales funnel looks more like a megaphone.

So, instead of your buyer pipeline tapering into a funnel, you want a post-purchase relationship with your paying clients … so you can grow your loyal customer base.

You also want the things your business values … like credibility, trust, and profits … to continue growing bigger and bigger with time.

A Sales Funnel Should Speed Up Your Lead Generation And Sales Processes

You can influence how your buyers move through the funnel by focusing on the most important places where they drop out.

But if you don't understand the areas of your funnel where your buyers transition from one step to the next, you won't be able to offer them the best solution. And getting them to convert into paying customers depends on how effectively you share the information they are looking for.

And because you know the pain of missing out on sales, optimizing your funnel is one of the ways you can grow your customer base.

However, the sales funnel is inherently not customer-focused. And your buyers' purchase decision-making process doesn't always follow a straight path.

And despite your best efforts … in reality … the path you have mapped down your sales funnel isn't their journey to a buying decision. You see … each person who enters the funnel transitions through the phases at their own pace.

And so, relying exclusively on the sales funnel for your content marketing strategy won't work for two reasons:

1. The sales funnel is a vehicle for you. It is not customer-focused. Because it outlines all touchpoints entirely from your point of view. So it is not suited for any customer-centered strategy.

2. The sales funnel assumes that all buyers enter the funnel at the top and then follow a straight path as they permeate to the bottom. But in reality, each member of the 'Decision-Making Unit' moves through your touchpoints uniquely.

So, if you want your content marketing to work, just focus your approach on your buyers' experiences instead. Look at the entire buying process from their point of view. And align your content marketing efforts with their journey to buy.

This way … you will know how to deliver a continuum of customer-focused content at every step of the decision-making process.

Your Sales Funnel Is Not The Buyer's Journey

The buyer's journey is a marketing model that explains your buyers' experiences as they move through your sales funnel.

But unlike a sales funnel, the buyer's journey will help you figure out how to engage your buyers in a way that puts the customer first.

It incorporates significant touchpoints and everything your buyers do in the entire sales cycle. From gaining awareness about your brand to receiving a 'thank you for your purchase' email after a successful transaction.

According to Michael Brenner … CEO of Marketing Insider Group … *"The buyer's journey is nothing more than a series of questions that you must answer."*

So, how does the buyer's journey apply to the 'Decision-Making Unit'?

Members of the 'Decision-Making Unit' do not walk the journey together. Each person will walk the journey as an individual. However, their paths overlap. Because they are working collectively towards the same purchase decision.

And so, for each archetype, the journey starts when they experience a triggering event related to their 'Jobs-To-Be-Done'. But at that point, they are neither aware of your product nor in need of it.

However, each persona kicks off his journey when he becomes aware of the problem. He begins searching for a solution to a pain point that changes his situation.

The buyer's journey flows in steps that are complementary to the phases of your funnel. And so, as they become aware of, consider, and evaluate your product, they travel along a parallel path to your sales funnel.

So ... where do you start?

The first step in creating an effective buyer's journey is to know the pain points of the 'Decision-Making Unit'. This knowledge will give you insight into their subconscious minds.

Knowing their subconscious thinking and pain points can also help you map out the steps they have to take before they arrive at a buying decision. And instead of pitching, you must adopt the mindset of helping.

You can structure your buyer's journey touchpoints to improve the effectiveness of your marketing campaign. And make it an efficient process for your buyers. It allows you to reach your buyers at each stage of their purchase decision-making process.

The goal here is to nurture your buyers toward making a purchase decision. Help them identify, evaluate, and mitigate their core problems against available solutions. Provide value at every decision-making stage. And share content that resonates with their most pressing needs.

In a world that has gone digital ... thanks to the mass adoption of the internet ... when your buyers have a problem, they will search for answers online. And so, it's important to note that your buyers no longer perceive your company as the informational gatekeeper.

Now your buyers can access a vast repository of information at their fingertips … online. Unlike the time when marketers controlled the flow of information.

And as information has become ubiquitous … as has access to it … your buyers have become active participants in their buying process.

The balance of power in most sales conversations has now shifted from your sales rep to them. Given the ease with which they can pull up reviews, competitor products, and cost-efficient alternatives.

Search engines and social media platforms have become their informational gatekeepers.

And they will seek the best content with the right message to help find solutions to their problems. So aim to target your buyers through messaging to reach the right people at the right time with your content.

If done right, they will have your offer on their mind when the time to decide to buy arrives.

How the buyer's journey in your target audience unfolds will depend on your industry, business model, product pricing, and the people you want to buy from you.

And when it comes to influencing your buyers' consumption behavior, every single stage of their journey is crucial.

The Decision-Making Process For First Time B2B Purchases

In this case, the organization faces a new problem that has not arisen in the past. They have no previous experience buying this particular product. As a marketer, you can influence their buying situation by providing the persons in the Decision-Making Unit with the required information and persuading them that your solutions are the best to solve their problem.

But the actual purchase will involve multiple stakeholders (the DMU) who will work through a formal, organized, and professional buying process … from recognizing a problem to selecting a supplier … before investing their money in your product.

This process typically consists of a series of distinct, sequential stages culminating in a purchase, which is then followed by a post-purchase phase.

And so, business-to-business (B2B) transactions take a little more time to reach the purchase decision. So it is not unusual for them to have very long sales cycles, often running into weeks or even months.

Here's why ...

First, most B2B products are complex, expensive, or both. Due to a lack of previous buying experience, the perceived risk associated with a new purchase is high. As a result, buying decisions are more critical, deliberate, and not impulsive, as lots of new information is needed. It takes time for it to be assimilated.

Secondly, the buying process in many organizations has multiple reviewing stages. Purchasing decisions are not the responsibility of one person. It is the norm to find a multi-person 'Decision-Making Unit' involved in the review and purchase approval processes. And since each team member will want to give their input and make their voice heard in every purchase, the process takes even longer before decisions are made.

And as a rule of thumb, the bigger the ticket value, the longer the sales cycle will be.

So, your prospects will expect you to give them enough information about your product at each step of the buying process. They will then review that information before they make an informed buying decision, which is called a considered buying decision.

What that means is that B2B companies have a protracted Decision-Making Process. It takes a little more time for them to arrive at a buying decision. And since, on average, their sales secure higher ticket buys than B2C sales, it might take 6 months, 12 months, or even longer to arrive at buying decisions.

Between a company's first realization that they need a product or service and the final decision to buy, is a complex, multi-step process.

Here are the 10 stages of the buying decision-making process that run parallel to the 10 content marketing goals discussed in an earlier chapter of this book.

Stage #1: *ATTENTION … Assessing The 'Jobs-To-Be-Done'.*

Your potential buyers are defining, categorizing, and capturing their needs. They are looking for your product or service to get the job done. But they have a problem they are unaware of. 'The Initiator', 'The Influencer', or 'The End-User' archetypes of the 'Decision-Making Unit' come across your content pieces, and their attention gets piqued. They want to know what's in it for them.

Your marketing goal is to influence them so they can recognize their problem.

Use empathy in your content to trigger their subconscious mind.

Address their needs from their perspective. It will then become clear to you why they buy your products and services in the first place.

Stage #2: *INTEREST … Recognizing There Is A Problem Or Need.*

'The Initiator' experiences a psychological trigger that enables him to recognize that there is a problem. He recognizes that the unmet need warrants some action, but he doesn't know how to solve this problem. He may approach 'The Influencer' or 'The End-User' and get them interested in searching for relevant information.

Your goal is to boost your visibility online. And you will use search engine optimization (SEO) techniques to achieve that.

You want to use keywords to increase search engine visibility and drive organic traffic to your content.

Stage #3: *DISCOVERY … Discovering Your Brand.*

'The Initiator' or 'The Influencer' visits your website to discover more about your company. They want to learn more about your brand. They wonder about who you are and what your company is all about.

Your marketing goal is to increase your brand's awareness. And make a good first impression with your buyers.

Stage #4: *EVALUATION ... Defining Product Requirements & Comparing Available Solutions.*

'The Influencer' needs to find out how to solve this problem but doesn't know who has the best solution. He compares the available options and sets the criteria for evaluating alternatives. He needs evidence that supports vendor promises and will eliminate solutions that aren't a good fit.

'The Decision-Maker', 'The Blocker', and 'The End-User' may also need to see this information.

Your marketing goal is to generate consumer demand for your products.

Share Subject Matter Expert (SME) content and use case studies and consumer-generated content strategically.

Stage #5: *ENGAGEMENT ... Reaching Out For Engagement.*

'The Influencer' or 'The End-User' wants to build trust. They are looking for relevant information and trying to connect with your brand by engaging with your content. They are trying to see if you are a good fit for them. So they want to see if your business is relatable so they can build an emotional bond with your brand.

Your marketing goal is to engage your buyers as you show concern for their needs.

Provide engaging content that speaks to your buyers' needs.

Stage #6: *DESIRE ... Ready To Give Your Offer A Test Drive.*

'The Influencer' or 'The End-User' perceives your lead magnet as being of high value. It promises immediate gratification and focuses on their problem. 'The Influencer' and 'The End-User' are willing to trade their email addresses for access.

Your marketing goal is to generate leads by offering a valuable lead magnet.

Stage #7: *NEGOTIATION ... Selecting A Supplier.*

'The Influencer' and 'The Decision-Maker' seek to outline the purpose of a product's features and its functionalities.

'The Blocker' experiences feelings of doubt and needs reassurance. He steps back to verify some of his beliefs and looks for social proof to overcome his objections and find answers to his questions.

'The Decision-Maker' consults 'The Initiator', 'The Influencer', and 'The End-User'.

Your marketing goal is to overcome common sales objections.

You can do this by following up on your leads and showing that you are an expert who can help solve problems.

Stage #8: *DECISION TO BUY ... Justifying The Purchase.*

'The Decision-Maker' might conduct limited research on the solutions under consideration. He discovers an aspect of your product he didn't expect, and from here on, he can't live without it. He commits to a purchase decision, becomes a paying customer, and arrives at this decision following consultation with 'Legal and Compliance'.

Your goal is to generate sales revenue by sharing transactional information that will help you close more deals.

Stage #9: *POST-PURCHASE EXPERIENCE ... Getting To Know How Well Your Product Works*

'The End-User' may not know how to use your product. He reviews the performance of your product and may consult your resources for help setting up or installing the product. 'The Initiator' and 'The Influencer' may also have an interest.

Your marketing goal is to increase your Customer Lifetime Value (CLV) by boosting retention and loyalty.

You want to remarket your offer to encourage repeat purchases and improve customer retention. You also want to turn your one-time buyers into loyal customers.

Stage #10: *ADVOCACY … Becoming Your Brand Advocate.*

'The End-User' or 'The Influencer' enjoyed the experience of using your product. They become your brand advocate when they mention your product to peers in their professional affiliations.

Your marketing goal is to turn your customers into brand advocates by offering incentives they can use to bring in referrals.

Create programs and incentives that will turn them into brand advocates.

Many businesses consider a sale to be the most significant event of the buying process. However, it is important to keep in mind that decision-makers must go through at least 10 different stages of the buying process before they can buy.

And so, as an experienced marketer, you want to focus on that process so you can put the buyer front and center.

Knowing how that process unfolds can help you find new ways to add value and make your content more useful. And showing empathy for your buyer at every stage counts toward winning a purchase.

The Decision-Making Process For Straight Repeat Purchases

A straight rebuy is when a company orders the same products from the same supplier for the same amount. It represents the most common form of repeat buying within B2B purchasing.

Since the buyer has already done business with this particular vendor, they are less likely to do a lot of research on the supplier and product. So it's easier for the organization to think about the same solution they thought about the last time the problem happened.

And if the problem your customer has is a recurring one, they will use your solution often.

To keep customers coming back, you need to keep the quality of your product or service high and make it easy for them to reorder. This will save them time. As a result, you will have a steady, consistent revenue stream.

The Decision-Making Process For Modified Repeat Purchases

A modified rebuy is when a business that has bought from you before wants to place another order, but they need to change a few things, like the specifications of the product or the terms of the purchase and delivery.

Because of this change, they will want to do more research and look over your product options, which could delay a future order.

They will also be looking to investigate many other potential sources of supply.

Use this opportunity to your advantage and offer a better solution to the problem so that they may consider you for future purchases.

The Purchase Decision-Making Process Is Not Linear

While the traditional sales funnel assumes that all your prospects are captured at the top and move down in a straightforward process to the bottom, in reality, they are likely to enter your sales funnel at random points.

Some might begin their process on an influencer's site or after reading your post on social media. Sometimes the trigger to begin the journey may be found on a competitor's site or in a product review.

Some may enter early at the top of the funnel, others in the middle, or even join much later … right before they make a purchase decision.

Regardless of how they come into your sales funnel, what is certain is that they won't necessarily pass through it in a straightforward, sequential fashion … from top to bottom.

They won't necessarily start at point 'A' and move through all stages to the finish line in a predictable pattern. Instead, they will often take a back-and-forth, cyclical, and multi-channel journey.

And so, you must optimize your touchpoints in the myriad of places in the digital realm where your content is distributed to facilitate their buying process. Don't just focus on catching them at the top and hope they somehow filter down the rest of your funnel.

Customize every touchpoint by making value-driven improvements that keep each archetype of the 'Decision-Making Unit' in your sales funnel … as you gently nudge them toward a purchase.

Your Buyers Complete 2/3 Of Their Decision-Making Process Before They Engage Your Sales Department

According to a 2013 study by the CEB Marketing Leadership Council … in partnership with Google … your prospects will complete at least 57% of the buying process before they engage your sales department.

What does this mean for your marketing?

It means that for the majority of your buyers' purchasing process, they are out there … all on their own … with minimal input from you.

They are building requirements and learning technical specifications. They are narrowing down their options and forming opinions. They are looking for timely information to help them make informed buying decisions.

This period is critical because this is when they figure out what they need, regardless of the actual product. You have a tremendous opportunity to get in front of them before they enter the 'buying window' … so you can shape the way they view potential solutions.

According to *"The Digital Evolution in B2B Marketing"* report … if your company fails to show up strong when your buyers need information, you'll be underserving them. You will be at risk of losing a sales opportunity.

But the question is … whose content are they consulting to shape most of their purchase decisions? How visible is your content when they search for answers online?

The success of your marketing campaigns depends on your ability to reach your prospects through the channels they prefer. To attract and hold their attention with information that removes the obstacles that hold them back.

And to help them achieve their 'Jobs-To-Be-Done' targets.

And so, as a forward-thinking marketer, you need to know where your buyers hang out to self-diagnose their problems. So you can align your content distribution to dominate those spaces.

Thus, knowing the decision-making process will help you tailor your content to show empathy for your buyers at each stage.

The B2B Purchase Decision-Making Process Thrives On A Continuum Of Empathy-Based Educational Content

The essence of your content strategy should come from the belief that you are there to help your buyers … not to serve yourself.

So you must recognize that different 'Decision-Making Unit' archetypes will need different kinds of information … depending on the buying stage they are in.

And when you have a deep understanding of what they need, you can create targeted and personalized content.

So you must think of your content as a body of work that delivers a continuous stream of information. A library where your buyers can search, discover, and consume knowledge on an as-needed basis.

You want to provide your buyers with relevant material that aids their decision-making. So consider your messaging, media selection, and content distribution timing at every stage of your buyer's journey.

And by ensuring maximum engagement at every stage, your content continuum sets the stage for you to meet your buyers where they are. Where you can maintain the continuing conversation your buyers want to have.

So start by thinking about how all the pieces of content fit together in your marketing campaign. Think about how you can serve your beginner, intermediate, and advanced buyers.

Create a content continuum that delivers escalating value at each touchpoint … rather than sharing random individual assets.

Your expertise will help your buyers go from knowing nothing about your business to liking your brand. And when you educate them about how they can solve their specific problems, you can drive momentum toward a purchase.

And as they travel along the buyer's journey, you want them to conclude that your company is the ultimate choice to help them solve their problems.

They eventually trust you and find it easy to select your brand.

You want a stream of content that works as a companion that your buyers can consult at each stage of their decision-making process.

The Key Takeaways from Chapter 7:

1. Your sales funnel is a vehicle for you. It outlines all touchpoints entirely from your point of view. So it is not suited for any customer-centered strategy.

2. The buyer's journey is a marketing model that represents the experiences your buyers have while interacting with your brand.

3. Understanding how decision-making unfolds can make or break your content marketing approach. It can help you find opportunities to tailor your content to show empathy for your buyers at each stage.

4. B2B decision-making includes both emotional and rational motivations for individual-level and company-level needs.

Coming Up In The Next Chapter ...

Top-Of-The-Funnel (TOFU) content.

CHAPTER SIXTEEN

Top-Of-The-Funnel (TOFU) Content

Quote

"Your top-of-the-funnel
content must be
intellectually divorced from
your product but
emotionally wed to it."

~ Joe Chernov ~
Chief Marketing Officer - Pendo.io

Every purchase decision-making process begins with an unmet need. And at the top-of-the-funnel (TOFU), your prospective buyers just realized they have a problem that they must solve.

'The Initiator' archetype of the 'Decision-Making Unit' is the person who will act first. Often, this means turning to Google to look for their problem.

But notice that he is not looking for your solution.

So, instead of trying to sell your product or service in the early stages, your content should create awareness.

How?

As it turns out, early-stage buyers will be gathering information. And you will have little direct involvement in their activities at that point. But you want to capture them during their quest.

The best you can do is create TOFU content that educates them to recognize their problem and helps them answer common questions.

And if you want to reach a wide range of potential buyers, your TOFU content strategy should cast the widest net.

Who should you focus on?

'The Initiator', 'The Influencer', and 'The End-User'

At this stage, they are agnostic about information sources. So the goal of your content strategy should be to draw them in. To shape their opinion.

Ideally, you want to position your content to grab their attention, increase brand awareness, and start building a relationship. You can use simple keywords to direct more traffic to your site.

At the top-of-the-funnel, your prospects will pass through three stages of the purchase decision-making process.

ATTENTION: The 1ˢᵗ Decision-Making Stage

In the first decision-making stage, your buyers are assessing their 'Jobs-To-Be-Done'. They are unaware of the problems they may have. And so you have to help them identify their challenges so they can prioritize the opportunity you will present.

So your goal here is to influence them to recognize their problem.

And since they are looking for what's in it for them, make sure to call out their problems and pain points early in the process. You have the unique opportunity to provide resources to help them define these problems.

Your potential buyers have early-stage search queries and are still trying to learn more about their 'Jobs-To-Be-Done'.

So use the fact that they are interested in what you have to say to capture and hold their attention.

And once you succeed in drawing them into your sales funnel, you want them to remain there and travel the entire journey to a purchasing decision.

But first … they must access your content.

The best way to get it seen passively is to seed it in locations where your buyers naturally spend their time online. You can make it easier for them to find it by distributing it to their favorite channels on different online platforms.

This is where you must think about using the following 4 attention-grabbing pieces:

Advertisements: *Ads are a classic marketing tactic for grabbing attention.*

> For most businesses to grow, the one thing they need most is traffic. And the fastest way to get more visitors to your content is through advertising.
>
> Ads work both as promotional and marketing activities. They can increase familiarity and trust between your brand and your buyers.
>
> A great Ad will use compelling copy to drive tons of traffic. And

instead of pitching, you can share enticing information about how your solution can help solve their problems.

And if potential buyers see multiple ads from you, they will start to warm up to your brand and consider you trustworthy.

Going by Google's 2022 Economic Impact Report, your business stands to make an average return on investment of $8 for every $1 spent on Google Ads. Not bad!

Advertorials: *An advertorial is a form of marketing ad.*

It mirrors the format of an objective editorial article.

But unlike traditional ads, advertorials read like legitimate and independent news stories.

And because people believe in and connect with news stories, advertorials are set in a more persuasive format. They are informative and help your audience understand your offer.

The goal is to use them to attract as many of your readers as possible to the top of the funnel.

Books: *A book is a long-form content piece on a topical subject.*

To write and publish a book on a subject, you have to have a certain level of expertise. This makes it a great way to display your credibility and authority.

As a long-form content piece on a topical subject, a book works as a multi-purpose marketing tool that can help you get attention.

You can use it to improve your visibility and get publicity through extensive media coverage.

Press Releases: *Press releases are official statements to media outlets.*

They are preferentially issued to disseminate news online rather than in print.

And because they go through established outlets, using keywords can help amplify your communication.

Also, online visibility will allow you to build quality backlinks that will give you great exposure. And that can help you expand your market reach exponentially for a few hundred dollars.

INTEREST: The 2nd Decision-Making Stage

In the second stage of the decision-making process, your buyers become aware that they have a problem. They experience psychological triggers that make them recognize their unmet needs.

This warrants some action, but they still don't know how to solve these problems.

Before they get to purchase anything, the first thing they will do is go to Google to research it ... and then compare it to equivalent products.

So they begin to search online.

They will search for specific words to get Google to provide them with the right information and answers that will help them solve their problems ... often without thinking twice about the search terms they type.

This is referred to as 'search intent'. Google makes it its priority to provide the closest possible content in the search results to what it believes the user intended to find.

And because they are searching online, your goal is to boost your search engine visibility. So you want to use the keywords they are likely to type into Google and incorporate them into your content for Search Engine Optimization (SEO).

You want to ensure that your content and SEO strategies match what your potential buyers are looking for when they type in those searches.

Improving your search engine rankings will boost your online visibility and get your content listed high in the results. If you rank highly in search results, you will notice an increase in the flow of organic traffic to your content.

In turn, your articles, blog posts, and podcasts will pop up whenever your buyers Google their problems. And if they can find you, more people with similar needs will also track your content online.

This is where you must think about using the following content assets:

Articles: *Articles are medium-length content assets.*

> They are objective editorial pieces that use a formal journalistic style to inform. They steer clear of personal opinion while presenting facts, figures, reportage, or statistics.

> And because articles go through a thorough editing cycle, they are error-free and accurate.

> Depending on the publisher, the standard length of your article can range from 1500 to 5000 words. Although it's usually somewhere in the former range.

> You can publish them in newspapers, magazines, and other traditional paper-style media ... including online versions.

> And when you focus on educating your prospects, you can build trust and increase the flow of traffic to your site.

Blog Posts: *Blog posts are short-form essays of 300 to 1000 words.*

> They are popular in content marketing because they show up when your buyers search for their problems online.

> Blogs describe things from a personal perspective in commonly used language. And you require minimal external editing.

> They often present the author's opinion and rely less on reportage and data.

> And because they live on your website, they continue to attract traffic to your site.

> Data from 1,531 HubSpot customers found that companies that maintain a blog have far better marketing results. On average, they

have 55% more visitors, 97% more inbound links, and 434% more indexed webpages.

They have also boosted Google search rankings.

Interviews: *Interviews happen on radio, TV, or online.*

An interview is a structured conversation in which one person asks questions and the other answers them.

An interview can put a human face on your brand. Hosting an interview with a subject-matter expert is an opportunity for great publicity.

And when you get interviewed as a guest on a talk show, you can get exposure that will allow you to connect with a new audience.

This increases your brand's visibility and can generate renewed interest in your products.

Podcasts: *A podcast is an audio medium used for topical discussions.*

As a marketing tool, it creates value because it is informative and educational.

And because a podcast is easy to consume, it can help you hyper-target your audience using keywords, meta tags, and metadata.

This will boost your traffic and SEO rankings and increase your discoverability online. Adding a description to each episode will help search engines understand your conversations ... and recommend them.

Hence, podcasts promise a good return on investment because they boost your webpage rankings.

DISCOVERY: The 3rd Decision-Making Stage

There are people in your target market who don't know your brand. They're not aware that your offer can solve their problem. But if your buyers make it to this point, you stand a great chance of holding onto them.

In the third decision-making stage, they want to learn more about you.

Many may not have heard of your company before, but they are curious enough to seek you out. So they track your website.

Brian Carroll, author of "*Lead Generation for a Difficult Sell,*" says ... "*Up to 95% of people who visit your website are just looking around. They are there to do research but are not yet ready to speak with your sales representatives. Nevertheless, up to 70% of them will eventually make a purchase, either from you or from one of your competitors*".

Thus, your goal is to leave them with a good first impression and create awareness about your brand.

Better still ...

Leave them with a lasting impression. That is the only thing better than a good first impression. So go out of your way to impress them by delivering targeted educational content.

Brand awareness is a crucial foundation that will enable you to acquire customers. Awareness establishes trust and creates positive associations. And it builds equity that allows your brand to become a consumer staple.

Here are some content options that you can use at this stage ...

Video Marketing: *Using videos to promote and market your product or service.*

Online video is huge. A medium that's highly preferred by web users. Much more than plain text. So incorporate it into your marketing to communicate your message more effectively.

A professionally written script can bring a topic to life and deliver your message in the shortest time possible. It can win over your viewers and help you get your message across in a way that is clear, creative, and natural. But a good hook will serve as the cornerstone of your message.

186

According to aimClear, a video search result has a 41% higher click-through rate than a plain text result ... an indication that your audience finds value in your content.

In another study, Forrester Research found videos to be 50 times more likely to boost organic ranking on Google than plain text.

The video content format is very popular with online visitors to websites. They will stay 2 minutes longer on your webpage if you feature an engaging video on it.

Also, videos positively improve your SEO results and speed up a customer's decision-making.

Peer-Reviewed Publications: *This is a formal part of scientific communication.*

Peer-reviewed publications help validate your research output.

So when you develop products based on research, you can always cite your publications to claim authority.

Authority can boost your brand's reputation. And make you stand out from your competitors by assuring your audience of the quality you bring to the market.

PowerPoint Presentations: *PowerPoint presentations use branded slide decks.*

They allow your team to present easily digestible visuals to a live audience. This can help you translate complex ideas, facts, or figures.

Your presentation script should be engaging. You want to communicate complex ideas using easily digestible visuals. This will captivate your audience's attention and help you capture their imagination. You want to elicit desire by showing the audience how they can benefit.

Your PowerPoint presentation can put a thought-provoking quote on a slide, tell a meaningful story, and hold people's interest.

You can add pictures, graphics, text, and videos to your

PowerPoint and show off your business in the best light.

And at the end of your presentation ... spur them into action.

Your sales team can also use your presentations to impress leads, potentially turning them into clients.

Website Content: *Your website is the digital home of your brand.*

And your website copy is your online sales rep.

Studies show that if a visitor to your website learns something from your site, it establishes your site itself as an authoritative source on the topic. That visitor may end up coming back to your website ... and will likely convert later, when they are ready.

When visitors arrive on your site for the first time, knowing little or nothing about your brand, they should feel pain if they leave without heeding your call to action.

Without the right words, your website is like a brand-new engine without fuel. Stunning to look at, but leaves you stuck in a jam.

And so, when someone lands on your page, your website copy must explain your brand to them.

They expect easy navigation. They want to find relevant content. But if your key messages don't appeal to their interests, they will bounce.

The content on your website needs to set early expectations for your value proposition. So, set it up to support your marketing goals. And lay out each page as a potential entry point for your buyers.

The Key Takeaways from Chapter 9:

1. At the top-of-the-funnel, your buyers are in the awareness stage.

2. In the 1st stage of the buying decision-making process, they are unaware of their problem. So your goal here is to influence them to recognize their problem.

3. In the 2nd stage, your buyers experience psychological triggers that make them aware they have a problem. They start to search for a solution online. And so, your goal is to use keywords and SEO techniques to increase the organic search visibility of your content.

4. In the 3rd stage, your buyers want to learn more about your brand. Your goal is to give them a great first impression of your brand and build awareness.

Coming Up In The Next Chapter ...

Middle-of-the-funnel (MOFU) content.

CHAPTER SEVENTEEN

Middle-Of-The-Funnel (MOFU) Content

Quote

"To build a long-term
successful enterprise, you
don't close a sale. You open
a relationship and make a
customer."

~ Patricia Fripp ~
Speaker & Business Presentation Expert.

The middle-of-the-funnel (MOFU) content belongs to the consideration stage. The content you share here acts as the bridge that closes the gap between initial intrigue (at the top-of-the-funnel) and purchase intent (at the bottom-of-the-funnel).

At this stage, you must put in the work to build trust-based relationships with your prospects. You also want to ensure that your value proposition sets you apart from your competitors.

These two elements could be the factors that decide whether or not a sale happens at the decision stage, which comes later.

The people you are targeting are already in your sales funnel. They have already recognized their unmet need, and now they are just looking for potential solutions that would serve them most effectively.

But who are they?

1. The new leads that you attracted to the top-of-the-funnel, and
2. Your current customers, who may be interested in a repeat purchase.

In the middle-of-the-funnel, you want to make sure that your content speaks to both sets and helps move them along to the next stage.

You also want your content to qualify them, help them self-select, and determine whether your offer is a good fit for them. And that's a good thing.

Why?

These people are searching for precise answers to their problems. They want information that will help them evaluate the merits of alternative solutions. So if you can filter out those not interested in your offer, you can concentrate your nurturing efforts ... in the next phase ... only on those most likely to buy from you.

But which members of the 'Decision-Making Unit' should you talk to primarily at this stage?

'The Influencer' archetype. This is the subject-matter expert.

He needs information to set the criteria for evaluating different approaches to solving their problem. And he should provide resources to better argue your case.

Why?

In his role in the 'Decision-Making Unit', he will typically consult 'The Decision-Maker', 'The Blocker', and/or 'The End-User' for their opinion. So if your content is not persuasive, educational, and targeted, it won't be convincing.

At this point, your prospects will pass through two more stages of the buying decision-making process.

EVALUATION: The 4th Decision-Making Stage

In the fourth decision-making stage, your buyers must define product requirements. They want to find information that sets the criteria for comparing the available options.

They commit to conducting research and evaluating alternatives.

This is where they start looking at specific brands with solutions that could potentially help solve their problems. So they need evidence to support vendor promises.

They don't know which solution is best. So they want to eliminate products that are not a good fit.

Your goal is to generate consumer demand for your products. And if you want to show them that you are a good fit, you must focus your content on educating them.

You want them to see you as a recognized industry expert. So you must resort to heavyweight content that builds your authority and positions you as the go-to brand.

These are the types of content that can win them over ...

Case Studies: *Case studies tell customer success stories in 1,500 words.*

People love to read and connect with stories about other people. And so when your customers say something, it means everything to your market.

There's no better way to tell your business success story than by letting your happy customers show quantitative outcomes that paint a picture of what success looks like for them.

And so the best conversion stories you can share with your prospects are those that your happy customers tell. This is a powerful tactic that can help you get around objections by appealing to your buyer's logical side of the brain.

That's why Sam Balter, Sr. Marketing Manager of HubSpot Podcasts, said ... *"Nothing sticks in your head better than a story. Stories can express the most complicated ideas in the most digestible ways"*.

A case study tells your customer's success story. It describes how your product helped one of your customers overcome a challenge.

Thus, a case study presents social proof that your customers are satisfied with your product and have a positive experience using it.

You can leverage the story-based structure to create empathy with your prospects so they can relate to people who have similar problems to their own.

This can help boost your conversion rates.

Product Catalog: *A document that lists all products or services you offer.*

A product catalog is a printed marketing asset that lists all the products or services you offer. It helps document difficult-to-memorize product information like technical specifications, features, price, and even color.

It serves as reference material and works well as a marketing asset that empowers your buyers to compare your products with those of other vendors.

It enhances a user's experience by making it easier for them to pick the most suitable option for their needs. It helps move your buyer one step closer to a purchase.

To set you apart from the competition, you can design your catalog with your brand colors, images, logo, and font family.

Product Description Webpage: *A web catalog of your e-commerce products.*

Your product description webpage is the virtual real estate that displays your offer. Its sole purpose is to showcase your products and explain the value you bring to potential customers.

It can have images from multiple angles and videos to show how your products look and function. But for B2B marketing, images only go so far.

What you need is well-written copy that will appeal to the subconscious senses and make all the difference between a sale and a lost opportunity.

And if the copy is done right, it almost becomes a feature of the product itself. It lists features, specifications, prices, payment options, and even reviews. It will enhance the buyer experience, not leave any questions unanswered, and facilitate buying.

And because the product description webpage lives on your company's website, it must serve as a virtual sales rep. This matters substantially in converting buyers because it will help you stand out from competitors.

You don't want to derail a sale or make shoppers abandon the purchase and your site. So you can link this page to supporting information from your blog to help your buyers make informed decisions.

And of course, product description copy has SEO benefits too.

Repurposing Peer-Reviewed Publications: *Transforming content into many formats.*

If you innovated a product based on the research you already published, you should communicate that in your marketing content.

Repurposing involves reformatting and reusing your original data by presenting it in new ways.

For example, you could write a white paper based on your publication. You could take information from your white paper to create an infographic that you can later post to another website. You could also use that data to write a blog post or turn graphics into social media images.

All you have to do is reposition data sets that can stand alone and create content around each sub-topic.

When you repurpose content on the same topic for different platforms, you can reach and connect with new audiences and generate demand for your products.

Subject Matter Expert Content: *Also known as thought leadership content.*

A 'subject matter expert' (SME) is someone with a depth of experience in a given industry.

SMEs have a lot of opinions and thoughts that can offer valuable perspectives on the solutions buyers need. A savvy marketer could pick their brain and create higher-quality thought leadership content for you.

Thought leadership can boost your content marketing programs. And because SMEs inject a dose of credibility, you could turn their opinions into persuasive content assets.

So when you share this kind of content, you position your brand as the recognized authority in your industry. That will get your target audience to develop an interest in your products.

ENGAGEMENT: The 5th Decision-Making Stage

In the fifth stage of the decision-making process, your buyers get to the point where they need to interact with you to forge trust. They are reaching out for engagement and want to see if your business is relatable and if you are a good fit for them.

Remember to be mindful of how your competitors show up in the marketplace and how they influence perception.

When you focus on educating your buyers, something amazing happens. You will position yourself as the 'problem solver', not the 'product seller'.

Your buyers begin to form an emotional bond with your brand. And that's good. Because an emotional connection is powerful. After all, people buy for emotional reasons. So this can make a huge difference in your content marketing.

According to the Harvard Business Review, emotionally engaged buyers will give you 52% more lifetime value. Because they tend to be more satisfied.

They are loyal, much less price-sensitive, and three times more likely to repurchase. They are also at least three times more likely to recommend your product or service and are less likely to shop around.

Your goal here is to engage with your buyers and show concern for their needs.

Some forms of interactive content can allow your buyers to personalize their experiences and get direct feedback.

For greater buyer engagement, use the following content assets …

Chatbots: *To engage with your buyers on your website.*

> A chatbot is an application that delivers a step-by-step conversation with your website visitors. It takes them through tunnels that instantly answer their questions.

> It serves as a virtual assistant that gives them quick information and answers throughout your buyer's journey. This boosts instant

engagement with your site visitors and may persuade them.

And when you deliver a positive experience, it helps to create an emotional link with the user that feels natural.

With so much of the world leaning towards automation, it's no wonder that bots have taken over the content marketing space.

And remember, the chatbot lives on your website and doesn't sleep. It turns up for duty 24/7/365.

Quiz Marketing: *Quizzes use guided questions and promise self-discovery.*

Quiz marketing is a tactic that uses well-defined questions to gather primary data about participants.

The funnels work well because they use powerful hooks that play right into the target audience's pain points and grab user attention.

That's why leading brands with the biggest lists use them. They gather quality feedback and feed user-generated insights into their marketing campaigns.

However, the interactive format is what attracts users in the first place. It is engaging and answers their questions in the right way.

For example, a self-assessment quiz can help a CEO discover how well his company performs against set criteria.

The 4 main advantages of marketing quizzes include...

1. Lead generation. By withholding the results until the user provides their email address, you can grow your email list.
2. Market segmentation. The quiz takers' responses can help you pre-qualify them and segregate them into groups.
3. Backlinks. Quiz funnels create quality backlinks that boost organic traffic to your site.
4. Cost-effective. You get all this at a fraction of the cost of regular lead-generation methods.

Social Media Posts: *Social media are virtual spaces for shared communication.*

The platforms offer relaxed and relatable ways through which you can talk to your buyers.

One advantage of posting on social media is that you can track the impact you have on your market through engagement metrics like views, likes, comments, follows, shares, mentions, and even hashtag use.

You can also use advanced algorithms to reach your target audience. If you use social media marketing well, you can reach a large number of people and get them more interested in your brand.

How many?

According to data from Statista, worldwide social media viewership stood at 3.6 billion people in 2020. This number is likely to increase to almost 4.41 billion in 2025.

The Key Takeaways from Chapter 10:

1. The middle of the funnel is the consideration stage. Your goal is to generate consumer demand for your products.

2. In the 4th decision-making stage, buyers must evaluate and compare available options. They want to find information that sets the criteria for evaluating alternatives.

3. In the 5th decision-making stage, your buyers get to the point where they need to interact with you to forge trust. They are reaching out for engagement and want to see if your business is relatable and if you are a good fit for them.

Coming Up In The Next Chapter …

Bottom-of-the-funnel (BOFU) content.

CHAPTER EIGHTEEN

Bottom-Of-The-Funnel (BOFU) Content

$$\mathcal{Q}uote$$

"I like to think of sales as
the ability to gracefully
persuade, not manipulate a
person or persons into a
win-win situation."

~ Bo Bennett ~
American screenwriter and Author of
"The Concept".

The bottom of the funnel (BOFU) is the decision stage. This is where all the buying interests of the individual personas in the 'Decision-Making Unit' intersect. And so when people arrive here, they must make one of two choices … to buy or not to buy.

The reason you created all of the other content in the earlier stages was to make sure you were supporting your prospects and helping them along the way … so they could convert. Now is the time to seal the deal.

How?

Your engagement with them at this stage is mostly transactional. So you want to put out content that will help you maximize your conversion rates and close more sales.

And since you have goodwill from the value you put into the earlier stages of the buyer's journey, you're now allowed to ask them to place a purchase order.

At this point, the subconscious thinking of your buyers is having a significant impact. And each 'Decision-Making Unit' archetype has a good idea of the kind of solution they want.

The only thing they have left to do now is choose a vendor.

So 'The Decision-Maker' takes steps to make a final decision. He becomes emotionally engaged with their pain points and is ready to seal the deal and buy.

But he must convince 'The Blocker' archetype beyond a shadow of a doubt that your product is the best option available to solve their problem.

So this is where your BOFU content must address the most common sales objections likely to arise and seamlessly usher them toward a sale. It will also help your case to have content that answers 'Legal and Compliance' questions about your offer.

At this decision stage, your buyers will pass through three more stages of the buying decision-making process.

DESIRE: The 6th Decision-Making Stage

In the sixth decision-making stage, your buyers are ready to give your offer a test drive.

They perceive your lead magnet to be of high value because it promises to give them something right away. It promises immediate gratification and focuses on their problem.

Your business goal is to generate leads. You want to strategically gate your lead magnet and collect your buyer's contact information ... say an email address ... in exchange for access to your content asset.

A lead magnet is a free giveaway. But it comes with a condition ... that your buyers share their contact information before they can access it. The most effective lead magnets are the ones that have a perceived high value and promise an irresistible instant reward.

As a marketing tool, it is a persuasive resource that will enable you to grow your email list. It puts your buyers in a position where they will be willing to exchange their email for your content that otherwise isn't available.

Once they surrender their email address, they have permitted you to reach out to them. And so later, you can follow up with nurturing email messages and progressively nudge them toward an actual purchase.

Here are some suggestions of what you can offer as lead magnets ...

eBooks: *An eBook, short for electronic book, is a short digital book.*

>An eBook is a great evergreen content asset that gives you one of the best opportunities to educate your audience.

>You can easily put one together by repurposing published data or expanding upon your existing blog content. You can also use them to share compelling proof that your product offers a viable solution for your buyer's pain points.

>Depending on your industry and marketing goals, you can deep dive into any topic to build your authority and increase credibility.

>eBooks are one of the most popular types of lead magnets because

they convert so well. Their length, format, and embedded visual elements make them a compelling choice for a lead magnet.

How-To Guide: *A document with step-by-step instructions that outline a process.*

A how-to guide is an informative piece of content that gives instructions on how to complete a technical task. Your prospect will want to use this guide as long as it is free, easy to understand, and provides valuable information.

For example, you might want to give technical instructions for using a piece of software or technology. You can also use how-to guides to share practical ways to convey a skill about an active process.

One of the main reasons people go online is to search for answers to their problems. You can position your how-to guide to generate leads from tons of traffic to your site.

eLearning: *Short for electronic learning.*

eLearning resources make for convenient educational content. They are easy to access online, anytime, anywhere. You then deliver it via electronic media like computers, tablets, and even mobile phones ... as long as they have an internet connection.

Focusing your content on your buyers' pain points will help you build curiosity that improves the perceived value of your brand. And you can have a greater impact on buying decisions when you deliver targeted messages to a segmented audience.

Use eLearning in your content marketing strategy to teach your buyers the correct way to use your products. This can increase engagement, facilitate your customer onboarding process, and improve customer retention.

Free Trial: *An offer that gives free access to your product for a limited period.*

A free trial can take the form of full access for a limited time or limited functionality for a while. It grants temporary access to your product or service upon initial registration.

By allowing free use, you can show your prospects what your product or service can do. They get to experience using it … at no risk to them … before you require them to commit to buying.

And if your product is fantastic and your prospects come to rely on it, they will choose to upgrade to paying customer status rather than give up access.

This can present the perfect opportunity to generate leads and improve conversion rates.

Landing Page: *A landing page is a lead capture page.*

This is a standalone web page specifically designed to convert your web visitors into leads. But unlike all other website pages, landing pages lead your prospects to a specific offer and encourage them to take just one action.

The landing page takes the place of your virtual sales rep. A well-designed landing page should speak to your potential buyers' pain points. It should generate demand and guide your buyers through the decision-making process.

It should motivate them to take that single desired action.

Having a data collection form makes it conversion-optimized. This allows you to capture your visitor's information in exchange for the lead magnet. And when you include a compelling call-to-action, you can greatly boost your lead generation efforts.

Product Demonstration: *Demo for short.*

Nothing beats the touch-and-feel factor. Sometimes, being able to see, touch, and even smell a product makes it more desirable to a potential customer. Especially when it comes to experiencing the unique features of your product design.

That's what product demonstrations are for.

They will enable you to present the real-time performance of your offer to an audience.

And many people tend to prefer this to simply listening to a sales pitch. It's also a very effective way to address product-related concerns.

Typically, a physical or online demonstration favors visual or hands-on learners. Seeing your product in action in real-time can help them fully grasp its value and potential.

The categories of products suitable for demos include those that are new to the market or revised versions of older products. Or even a whole new category of products.

Just make sure you get your buyers to sign up for your demos. This gives you access to their contact details.

Webinar: *An educational seminar for an online audience.*

A webinar is one of the most effective audiovisual educational resources. It gives you the chance to communicate your value proposition and can leave a positive impact on your audience. This can help you build credibility with your audience.

You can simultaneously reach many online viewers in different time zones. Participants can log in from any location and receive information in real-time.

People who want to attend the webinar must register, put the date in their calendars, and set aside time for the event. They must show up at the right time and then give you 1 to 3 hours of their time.

But unlike watching a video, where the viewer can pause it and come back at any time, a webinar uses the power of scarcity. And so, if your prospects leave or miss the webinar, they will feel the pain of missing out.

This works in your favor to improve your conversion rates.

But the fact that it's free doesn't mean that your audience won't get value. You can showcase their problems and teach them how to

206

perceive value in your offer. You can also show them how to use your solution, attend to their objections, and answer their immediate questions.

This allows you to soft sell, which feels much more natural.

White Paper: *An authoritative report that simplifies a technical topic.*

A white paper presents expert knowledge on a topic and backs it up with statistics from reliable, aggregated sources.

Repurposing data from your original research can build your credibility. And the in-depth insights and expert-level content help position your brand as an industry expert.

And when you use visual elements like charts, graphs, and tables, you can simplify complex technical information.

The 2015 TechTarget Media Consumption Report says 91% of B2B buyers use white papers to research buying decisions.

But unlike short-form content like blogs, a white paper will elevate your brand. It will help you gain a competitive edge as an authority.

It will also help you generate leads and build thought leadership.

NEGOTIATION: The 7ᵗʰ Decision-Making Stage

When your buyers start warming up to your product or service, they will step back to verify some of their objections.

What's the first thing they're likely to do? One or both of the following:

1. Ask their peers whether they used your product or service. And if they have, whether they would recommend it.
2. Go online and research what others say about your product or service.

And so you should be aware that in the seventh decision-making stage, your buyers have sales objections they need to overcome. They want reassurance that if they select you as a vendor, they will have made a sound decision.

According to BrightLocal's Local Consumer Review Survey 2022, 99% of consumers look to peers on the internet to make a purchasing decision. They know that a little online research could spare them from a bad experience and poor use of their budget investment.

Your goal is to nurture them and help them overcome those objections. And the best way to handle their objections is to provide social proof.

So give them the following content assets to answer their questions. And make sure you provide the right information at the right time.

Email Marketing: *Content marketing via email.*

> Most of your prospects are never ready to buy the very first time they make contact with your offer. Not even when they become leads.
>
> Email is a unique platform that allows you to follow up with them and deliver your content to their inbox. You can speak to your directly signed-up audience at a time that is convenient for them.
>
> According to a 2019 report entitled *"101 Email Marketing Statistics Every B2B Marketer Should Know in 2022,"* 3.9 billion people used email in 2019. And that number was projected to climb to 4.25 by 2024.
>
> They also found that 86% of B2B professionals preferred to use email for business purposes.
>
> This is consistent with the findings of a study by OptinMonster, which indicates that more than 90% of people in the US have email addresses. And 99% of them check their inbox every day. Of those, 58% check their emails first thing in the morning.
>
> The best part is that email marketing remains one of the most cost-effective digital marketing strategies … with one of the highest returns on investment (ROI). It's affordable, allows for targeted messaging, and is easy to measure.
>
> A drip email campaign can help you build relationships with your leads. And you can create personalized and custom experiences to increase their engagement with your brand.

Email marketing also allows you to follow up with new customers and returning customers. And you can segment your list to send targeted nurturing messages geared towards converting them into paying customers.

One Sheets: *Single-sheet documents that showcase your product.*

Your business buyers often have objections or questions about your offer that they would like to think over. And sometimes your one sheet becomes a valuable content asset that often works as a reminder that you can place in their hands ... or share online as an email attachment.

Though it is small and portable, it allows you to compact a lot of information about your products into a small area. You can engage your audience by giving them adequate information to create enough interest.

You can either print on both sides of the sheet or design them as downloadable PDF documents.

They are perfect for trade shows and networking opportunities. They serve as a perfect introduction to your business. And you can use them to sell your brand and convey your message.

You can dispatch them to a variety of locations, including promotional giveaways. You can also send them through direct mail or place them on tables in your office.

Your prospects can take it and use it as a reference at a later time.

Sales Battlecards: *Also known as selling guides.*

A battlecard is a one-page sales tool that helps sales reps manage customer expectations and have better conversations with prospects.

It is made up of short pieces of copy that describe your product in a persuasive way that makes people want to buy it.

The most valuable thing about a battlecard is that it summarizes how your product stacks up against your competition in terms of performance and value. It also includes tactics such as industry pricing that can help you communicate your unique selling proposition.

A battlecard is a fantastic resource that your sales team can springboard off during in-person or phone conversations, as well as via email.

So, giving your sales reps access to this information during a sales negotiation can help them answer questions quickly, deal with sales objections, and talk with authority.

Sales Closing Call Script: *These are call scripts that guide sales conversations.*

Nowadays, most B2B sales teams are made up of young people in their 20s. They don't have years of experience behind them in the craft.

Your buyers want you to inspire them. And your role during a closing call is to lead the conversation.

A benefit of your closing script is that it helps keep your sales representative in control of his conversation with a prospect. It helps keep your sales rep on track and makes him appear prepared for any discussion.

Eventually, this will help your reps choose the right phrases to seal a deal and convey important information more effectively.

And because a closing call can make or break the sale, using a script allows you to duplicate the success of your best sales closers. This can help you improve the overall effectiveness of your closing rates.

DECISION: The 8th Decision-Making Stage

In the eighth decision-making stage, your buyers must justify their purchase decision.

They discover an aspect of your product they didn't expect. And from here on, they can't live without it. So they commit to buying.

Your goal is to generate sales revenue by easing the path to purchase. Show them what it will be like to work with you.

And remember not to forget to validate their decision.

Here are the content pieces for this stage ...

Business Proposal: *A persuasive sales letter outlining your value proposition.*

> A quality business proposal is an integral part of any successful deal.
>
> It is the formal document you send to a B2B-facing prospect to secure a business agreement.
>
> It is meant to draw in more, better, and higher-paying work from prospective clients.
>
> - It outlines who you are and what you can do for them.
> - It explains that you understand the problem they are facing.
> - It outlines the solution your company offers.
> - It provides an estimate of the resources required to implement the solution ... that is time, money, etc, and
> - It includes the 'Terms Of Agreement' that set clear expectations and describe how your company will implement this solution.
>
> Your proposal will promote your services and elevate you to a higher tier of clientele. It can make all the difference between losing a prospect and closing a client. Thus, it can make or break your chances of securing a new client.

So you have to write it in a way that speaks to your buyer's immediate needs and also explains why you're the best option for the job. Ultimately, it should persuade your prospect to do business with you.

Sales Page: *A sales page is a webpage with only one goal …*

… to convince your page visitors to click, register, call, or buy your offer.

That's it!

And the sales copy is what your potential customers will read. So you want to ensure that it leaves them feeling like what you're selling can solve their problem.

What should your sales copy do?

It should …

- Tell your page visitors why they need your product.
- Address their objections and help overcome them.
- Provide an offer so compelling that they can't say no.
- Have a clear call-to-action (CTA).

And the more copy you have on the page, the better the SEO benefits. Just be careful not to have information overload.

Testimonials: *Honest endorsements your customers give your product.*

Why do you need them?

Because your target audience has grown weary of sensationalized marketing claims. And generally, they don't trust your claims.

So who is best placed to be a more credible ambassador for your business?

A recent study by BigCommerce found that 72% of consumers are more likely to trust a business after reading positive reviews about it online. And in another study by Spectoos.com, customers are likely to spend 31% more on a business with good customer testimonials.

That's a huge endorsement you can leverage.

Testimonials are the voices of your most satisfied customers. They are honest endorsements of your product or service. They make a less aggressive sales pitch and can help you build trust and credibility.

And because they come from unbiased third parties, they are effective at highlighting your best selling points.

Aim to use testimonials with the most specifics. Those that address your buyer's pain points and touch on solutions that you know are key issues for your customers.

How do you get these?

Ask your best customers for testimonials that provide much-needed social proof. Ask specific questions to guide testimonials in the right direction, and be sure that the statements have an air of credibility.

Consider including names, ages, and even photos to increase the credibility of each testimonial.

Reputation is everything in business. So don't use fake endorsements. Because your customers can easily spot that. And remember that using fake testimonials can seriously damage your brand's trustworthiness.

Video Sales Letter (VSL): *A video designed to sell a product or service to viewers.*

Video sales letters use the same persuasive principles used in written sales letters. You can include a video sales letter on your homepage, landing pages, and digital ads.

Like the classic sales letter, your video sales letter should grab your viewers' attention. You want to display your authority, build trust, and provide value.

You should also talk about their pain points and show how your product can solve those problems. Don't forget to include a compelling call to action that will inspire action.

According to Wyzowl, people love video content and prefer to watch more videos than read text online.

But what does that mean for your content marketing?

Using video in your content marketing can help you build credibility and trust with your viewers.

Wyzowl also found that 86% of businesses use some form of video marketing to promote their brands and products.

So if you haven't joined the bandwagon yet, it is time to gear up!

The Key Takeaways from Chapter 11:

1. In the 6th decision-making stage, your buyers are ready to give your offer a test drive. They perceive your lead magnet to be of high value because it promises to deliver immediate gratification. It promises to help them understand how to solve their problem. Your business goal is to generate leads.

2. In the 7th decision-making stage, your buyers experience feelings of doubt and need reassurance. Your goal is to nurture them and help them overcome their objections.

3. In the 8th decision-making stage, your buyers discover an aspect of your product they didn't expect. From here on, they can't live without it. So they commit to a purchase. Your goal is to position your brand in such a way that when they search for a path to buy, they will find it right away.

Coming Up In The Next Chapter …

Revenue-optimization-of-the-funnel (ROFU) content.

CHAPTER NINETEEN

Revenue-Optimization-Of-The-Funnel (ROFU) Content

$$\mathcal{Q}uote$$

"If you don't take care of
your customers, your
competitor will."

*~ **Bob Hooey** ~*
Speaker, Business & Leadership
Success Author.

The classic sales funnel only promotes customer acquisition at three basic levels ...

- Top-of-the-funnel (TOFU),
- Middle-of-the-funnel (MOFU), and
- Bottom-of-the-funnel (BOFU).

But your content marketing approach should factor in an after-sales strategy. That's what revenue-optimization-of-the-funnel (ROFU) content is for.

You want to use it to support the growth of a loyal customer base in two ways ...

1. *Repeat customers.*

   This is where ROFU content supports post-purchase customer service. It must anticipate the 'Succeed Search Intent' and show your customers how to use your product or service.

   It must check in to verify your new buyer's satisfaction with their purchase. It must also influence your buyers to make repeat purchases.

2. *Word-of-mouth referrals.*

   A word-of-mouth referral is an organic way to acquire customers from the recommendations loyal customers make to their friends, peers, family, colleagues, or followers on social media ... because they have had positive customer experiences using your products or about your company.

   Not only is it highly valuable because it is free, but most people (83%, according to Nielsen.com) trust word-of-mouth recommendations.

Why Are Repeat Customers And Word-Of-Mouth Referrals Important?

Unlike the classic marketing approach that looks at your buyer pipeline as a tapering funnel, you want to have a post-purchase relationship with your paying clients. So you can grow your loyal customer base over time and create a modern sales funnel that looks more like a megaphone.

While customer acquisition efforts that capture new customers are not necessarily a bad thing, there are many advantages to having an after-sales content strategy that emphasizes customer retention.

And since you've already paid the acquisition cost, why not capitalize on your customers to scale your business?

Here are six ripple effects of a post-purchase content marketing strategy on your business ...

1. According to BIA/Kelsey LLC, for many businesses, 50% of annual revenue comes from repeat customers, and they spend 67% more than new customers.

2. "*Referral Marketing Statistics*" by Review42.com reported that leads referred to a business by happy customers are 4 times more likely to convert ... compared to those from other sources.

3. According to Bain & Company ... a management consulting firm ... repeat customers bring in 50% more word-of-mouth referrals than one-time buyers.

4. A Gartner "*Marketing Technology Survey*" found that 80% of a company's future profits will likely come from 20% of its current customers ... through repeat purchases and referrals.

5. Another study by the online marketing company Constant Contact Inc. found that it is 16 times more expensive to acquire new buyers than to have existing customers re-purchase more.

6. In a case study, Schmitt, Skiera, and Van den Bulte found that it costs far less to convince paying customers to buy again than to acquire a brand-new buyer.

That's why Bob Hooey ... Speaker, Business and Leadership Success Author, said ... *"If you don't take care of your customers, your competitor will."*

So any serious business should work hard to retain their valued customers.

In this final phase of your sales funnel, your buyers will travel through two stages.

EXPERIENCE: The 9th Decision-Making Stage

In the ninth decision-making stage, your first-time buyers may not know how to use your product. They will consult your resources for help.

Your goal is to improve their post-purchase experience and turn one-time buyers into loyal customers.

You want your customers to return and buy from you again in the future.

And so a good post-purchase experience can influence your customers to view your brand positively. A trustworthy and helpful brand has all the essential ingredients to promote customer loyalty.

Your after-sales content marketing strategy should include the content assets below ...

End-User Documentation: *This is a post-purchase user guide.*

> The individual who eventually uses your product or service is known as 'The End-User'. This isn't necessarily 'The Buyer' archetype of the 'Decision-Making Unit'.

> End-user documentation forms an essential part of your buyers' overall post-purchase experience. It should include resources that will guide your users through the installation process and help them successfully use your product.

> And if your product is more complex than a simple roll of paper towels, you must provide a user guide.

> End-user documentation should highlight why buyers need it rather than focus on product features. It should improve your

buyers' experiences, reduce your support costs, and improve sales results.

Show your buyers how they can troubleshoot as they perform tasks. Help them learn how to use your product properly … and get the most out of it.

Product literature should help you give your buyers the best experience. It should leave them feeling like you care for them rather than leave them feeling like you're only interested in their money.

When your buyers know that you care about them beyond their bank account, they are likely to return as loyal customers.

Include links to your website, tutorials, FAQs, and user forums to give your customers access to additional resources. Include a list of customer care phone numbers as well.

But your end-user document isn't just for new customers. Experienced customers may also refer to it from time to time to solve specific problems.

Frequently Asked Questions (FAQ): *The page helps customers troubleshoot.*

If your current or potential customers keep asking the same questions, you should consider creating a FAQ page on your site.

A FAQ page is a webpage that contains a non-exhaustive list of straightforward questions and answers. It will help you clarify the basics of your offer and general policies, among other things.

It covers the main concerns in a text-heavy manner. It also covers topics from your office hours to shipping and handling.

The FAQ page gives your visitors a central place to find answers. It will improve your users' experience by offering them an alternative to waiting on the phone for simple answers.

And so, having a FAQ page is a time-saving customer service tactic. Customer care staff don't have to answer calls individually. The FAQ page can also help you manage customer expectations and overcome objections.

And if you really want to drive internal page views that get people to look at other pages on your site, put links to those resources on your FAQ page.

You may want to know that search engines love FAQ pages. They carry long-tail keywords that boost Google search rankings. Thus, having a FAQ page is a great SEO strategy.

Knowledge Base: *A self-service online library about your products.*

According to the Harvard Business Review, long-term customers prefer to find solutions on their own before they reach out for help.

A knowledge base is a self-service customer education portal that addresses recurring issues. It is a resource that goes beyond what a FAQ page does. It improves the buyer experience by helping them handle more of the simple issues on their own.

This gives your front-line service reps more time to devote to addressing complex issues that take longer to handle ... that customers can't solve by themselves.

Your knowledge base should archive many forms of digital content, including ...

- FAQs,
- step-by-step process guides,
- introductory articles,
- video demonstrations,
- glossaries and definition lists.
- and so much more.

Thus, having great documentation in your knowledge base boosts SEO and helps you show up in search results.

This can eventually help you acquire new customers.

ADVOCACY: The 10th Decision-Making Stage

According to Tomoson's 'Influencer Marketing Study', advocacy is a marketer's dream ... cost-effective and high-yielding. And for every dollar spent on advocacy marketing, businesses earn a return of $6.50. That's a whopping 650% return on investment (ROI).

Not bad! But what is the explanation for such a high ROI?

That's because prospects referred to your business by your customers have a 37% higher retention rate ... according to 'The Value of Referral Marketing' report published by Signpost.

This makes advocacy one of the strongest customer acquisition strategies.

In the tenth decision-making stage ... the final stage of the buying decision-making process ... you want to bring in business referrals.

Your goal is to turn your customers into brand advocates by offering them incentives they can use to bring in business referrals.

You want your buyers to become raving fans who promote your business. You want them to tell others about your product and brand through social media, reviews, and word-of-mouth marketing.

So you improve the quality of the buying process and make sure they have a good post-purchase experience.

Start by requesting that your verified buyers leave customer reviews on product pages. You can also invite your clients to participate in case studies.

Always have your marketing team scout through social media for enthusiastic posts about your products or brand. You may be pleasantly surprised by customer creativity.

You can use that content strategically to generate buzz around your brand and products.

These are the types of content that serve customer advocacy well ...

Consumer-Generated Content: *Also called user-generated content.*

> Consumer-generated content is original, brand-specific content that your customers create organically. Not you.

> It can be anything from comments, reviews, videos, images, or posts published on social media or other channels.

> Research by TurnTo Networks showed that 90% of buyers look at consumer-generated content to help make buying decisions. This is more than they see in promotional emails or even search engine results.

> The 2015 *"Global Trust in Advertising"* report by Nielsen ... which surveyed more than 28,000 online users from 56 countries ... found that 92% of your potential buyers trust word-of-mouth recommendations over traditional advertising.

> To boost sales, you should let consumer-generated content do the selling. It works as social proof. It reassures your buyers and promotes your brand message.

Customer Reviews & Star Ratings: *Feedback shared by verified customers.*

> A customer review is the opinion of a verified customer who has used and experienced your product or service. Such opinions are usually left online on product pages.

> A star rating is a form of consumer review that grades quality. Whereas a 5-star rating stands for the best quality, a 1-star rating stands for poor quality.

> In the virtual space, reviews and star ratings play the same role as traditional word-of-mouth. They are impactful in endorsing your marketing message.

> You can take screenshots of them and leverage this content as social proof for your other content. For example, use them on your homepage, in email campaigns, or on landing pages.

> But how many reviews do you need to showcase your brand's reputation?

While there's no magic number to it ... according to BrightLocal's 'Local Consumer Review Survey 2022' ... 98% of consumers read product reviews. 77% of potential customers desire to read at least 2 or 3 reviews before making a purchase decision.

Not only do reviews improve conversion rates, but they also increase sales and improve the Google ranking of your website.

eNewsletters: *Email Newsletters.*

An eNewsletter is a periodic email that you use to share useful information. It's a great way to keep in touch with clients, prospects, and subscribers.

It can help you nurture leads and update your subscribers about your business, products, and services.

You can also use eNewsletters to assert your position as a thought leader by sharing industry trends. And incorporate educational content that informs your subscribers of the latest news, tips, or updates.

And, occasionally, you can share information about upcoming product launches and promotions ... giving your customers priority access.

eNewsletters are an important component of effective email marketing and branding. You have the added opportunity to convert leads that aren't quite ready to buy from you just yet.

Regular contact with your customers will help you create meaningful customer relationships. This will help you build trust and keep you top-of-mind.

A follow-up with eNewsletters might be all you need to turn missed opportunities into increased conversions.

The Key Takeaways from Chapter 12:

1. In the 9th stage of the decision-making process, your first-time buyers may not know how to use your product. They will consult your resources for help. Your goal is to improve their post-purchase experience and turn one-time buyers into loyal customers.

2. In the 10th decision-making stage, you want your customers to become brand advocates. You want them to promote your business through social media mentions, reviews, and word-of-mouth marketing. Your goal is to turn your customers into brand advocates by offering them incentives to bring in business referrals.

Coming Up In The Next Chapter ...

PART 5: Moving Forward. Next Steps.

Part 5

Moving Forward. Next Steps.

NEXT STEPS

What Are Your Options?

Here's what you can do next …

Option #1:   You are now armed with everything you need to take action, and I'm sure you've got a good grasp of the concepts presented. You can work on your own and apply the methodologies outlined in this book. I'll be pleased to see you put this knowledge to good use. At least that way, I'll have played a small role in helping you improve your content marketing campaigns.

Option #2:   If you haven't been lucky enough to have found a skilled copywriting partner who can adapt to different marketing assignments, and write in a style and tone that aligns with your brand, feel free to contact me for a consultation. We can set up a virtual meeting to establish if working with me is a good fit for you. I'd be honored to be a valuable member of your marketing team.

Do this …

Send your request to contact@lifesciencecopywriter.com or,

Visit our website at https://www.lifesciencecopywriter.com.

No matter which option you choose, getting started is the most important thing to do.

ABOUT THE AUTHOR
Juliette R. Ongus, PhD.

Juliette is a business-to-business (B2B) copywriter, a certified website content auditor, the founder of *Life Science Copywriter*, and a member of the *Professional Writers Alliance* (PWA).

She is a biomedical scientist, researcher, and university-level academic with an MSc in Biotechnology and a Ph.D. in Molecular Virology.

Having extended her career to finding innovative solutions for marketing communication, she developed an interest in initiatives that improve how life science businesses communicate with clients.

With 17+ years of industry experience under her belt, Juliette can comfortably say that she knows the needs of life science prospects … because she has been one.

Through first-hand experience, she gained a deep understanding of both life science products and customers. She's visited their websites, read their promotional content, and bought and used their products.

And now, as a B2B copywriter, she sees both sides of the equation. Your viewpoint and that of your prospects. That makes her uniquely qualified to help you write your sales copy and create marketing content that resonates with your prospects.

Should you need help with your copywriting projects …

Connect with her on LinkedIn at:
https://www.linkedin.com/in/juliette-ongus/

Or send an email to:
juliette@lifesciencecopywriter.com